66

BOOKS OF SEED

WINDEE D. DIXON

ISBN 978-1-0980-8030-3 (paperback)
ISBN 978-1-0980-8031-0 (digital)

Christian Faith Publishing, Inc.
832 Park Avenue
Meadville, PA 16335
www.christianfaithpublishing.com

Printed in the United States of America

CONTENTS

The Power of the Tongue and Seeds of Words

Every word that we speak is living and alive. Every word is a seed and will produce a fruit. It will either produce life or death. Death and life are in the power of the tongue and they that love it shall eat the fruit thereof. There is not one word that doesn't have life or a purpose. Whatever we speak will manifest, it will come to pass.

God shows us several illustrations and examples in the Word of God on how what we speak out of our mouths will produce either life or death. An example of God speaking *life* into existence can be found in Genesis 1:3 KJV, "And God said, 'Let there be light:' and there was light." We can see here that God spoke, He used His mouth to speak light into existence and then there was light. "And God saw the light, that it was good: and God divided the light from the darkness" (Genesis 1:4 KJV). After God spoke let there be light, there was light, and then it was seen in the natural realm, it was made manifest.

Another illustration on how our words are living and alive and can either produce the ending result of life or death can be found in Matthew 21:18–19 KJV with the withered fig tree. Let's look at Matthew 21:18–19 KJV, "Now in the morning as he returned into the city, he hungered. And when he saw a fig tree in the way, he came to it, and found nothing thereon, but leaves only, and said unto it, 'Let no fruit grow on thee henceforward for ever.' And presently the fig tree withered away."

These two illustrations give us a template of how words are powerful, how they manifest, and we are able to see the manifestation of what we have spoken. The question God has for you today is what are you speaking out of your mouth? God wants us to understand that we are created in His likeness and in His image. If He is a speaking Spirit, then so are we. If He speaks and things manifest, then so can we! We are spirits that have a soul and live in a body. We have been created in the likeness and image of God.

We are designed to speak and to create and to bring life, and we also have the power to bring forth death, doom, and destruction in our lives and in the lives of others. We have the power to change our situation with the Word of God, we have the power to change our atmosphere, and most importantly we have the power to change who we are with the words we speak.

With the words we speak, they can be keys to unlock our destinies. They have the power to create worlds. Mountains can be moved, the sea can part, and the storm can calm all in the power of the word that is spoken.

ILLUSTRATIONS AND EXAMPLES OF THE POWER OF THE TONGUE

It is imperative that we choose our words wisely, that we don't spew out the mouth everything that comes to our mind. Out of the abundance of the heart, the mouth speaks. Whatever that's in you will come out. The Word of God says, "Let no corrupt communication proceed out of your mouth, but that which is good to the use of edifying, that it may minister grace unto the hearers" (Ephesians 4:29 KJV).

On a deeper level, we have to understand that we have an adversary, the devil that goes about like a roaring lion looking to see who he may devour. Oftentimes, we think it's us that have these thoughts, but what the devil likes to do is to use the "I" or "I'm" statements in our thoughts, so we think it's us thinking these things, and when we end up speaking it out of our mouths, it brings on a snare; it brings on a trap.

James 3 provides several illustrations of the untamable tongue. "Behold also the ships, which though they be so great, and are driven of fierce winds, yet are they turned about with a very small helm, whithersoever the governor listeth" (James 3:4 KJV). James points out that during his era, large ships were driven by the fierce winds, but in order to change directions and or to turn, the large ship was maneuvered by a very small wooden rudder, wherever the pilot desires. What does that mean? That means that no matter what type of chaos you are experiencing, no matter how strong the storm is, you have the power to use your tongue, your mouth, to speak what you want to see manifest. James said wherever the pilot desires. So if you are not where you are desired to be, you have the power of your tongue to speak into manifestation what you desire!

"Even so the tongue is a little member, and boasteth great things. Behold, how great a matter a little fire kindleth! The tongue is so set among our members that it defiles the whole body, and sets on fire the course of nature; and it is set on fire by hell" (James 3:5 KJV). "But the tongue can no man tame; it is an unruly evil, full of deadly poison. Therewith bless we God, even the Father; and therewith curse we men, which are made after the similitude of God. Out of the same mouth proceedeth blessing and cursing. My brethren, these things ought not so to be. Doth a fountain send forth at the same place sweet water and bitter? Can the fig tree, my brethren, bear olive berries? either a vine, figs? So can no fountain both yield salt water and fresh" (James 3:8 KJV).

We have the power to set a fire with one word. We can bless and curse in one sentence. This according to James is abnormal. He goes on to say, "Does a fountain send forth at the same place sweet water and bitter? Can the fig tree, my brethren, bear olive berries? Either a vine, figs? So can no fountain both yield salt water and fresh." So that lets us know that we do have the power to tame our tongue by the power of the Holy Spirit. The rudder is the Holy Spirit, the bit in the mouth of the horse is the Holy Spirit. The Holy Spirit will heal our spring from bitter waters.

We need to allow the Holy Spirit to heal us, to heal our souls and hearts, and begin to pour in the Word of God in the bible that is filled with sixty-six books of seeds. There are sixty-six books in the *bible* to help us change for the better, to speak life and not death.

SCIENCE AND THE BRAIN

There has been extensive scientific research and studies to prove that when a person speaks negativity or speaks death that it has a negative chemical reaction to a person's brain—the person that the words are being spoken to—and their situation in life turns for the worse. As a person speaks negative words, the brain, in return, releases stress hormones that impair the neural connections in the brain. It targets problem solving and cognitive functions. The same goes when a person is speaking negatively and a person hears it.

Did you know that when you hold a positive word in your mind, the frontal lobe of your mind is stimulated? The frontal lobe is where memory, emotions, problem solving, social interaction, motor function, and impulse control function. It is known as the "control panel" of who we are when it comes to our personality and our ability to communicate. The frontal lobe is responsible for moving you into action.

As you think and concentrate on positive words and speak positive words, it will start to affect other areas in the brain. For instance, your parietal lobe will begin to change. In this area of the brain, your perception of yourself begins to change along with others that you talk to or have a relationship with. The parietal lobe processes your sensory information and your perception of things.

When you speak life into you, it does something for you spiritually and physically. It makes you feel more calm, more balanced, focused, and happier. Speaking negative takes more energy than speaking positive. In result, when you speak life, it helps you be more productive in life. When we constantly speak negativity or negative self-talk, it brings on anxiety, depression, high stress levels, and stagnation in your personal life and can even effect and bring stagnation in the lives of others around you.

There was a scientific study done by psychologists Mate S. Nieuwland and Gina R. Kuperberg from Tufts University. They did a study on measuring "event-related" potential responses (ERP) as the participants read statements. An ERP is an electrical brain response that is recorded by an electroencephalograph. The statements had midsentence words that made the statement true or false. When the participants read the affirmative statements, large ERPs happened specifically at the words that made the statement false.

Participants read pragmatically licensed or pragmatically unlicensed statements. Pragmatically licensed statements are informative statements and sound natural. Pragmatically unlicensed statements are unnatural statements and are not helpful. An example of a pragmatically licensed statement would be, "With proper equipment, scuba diving is very <u>safe</u> and often good fun." Do you see the underline word in this sentence? The midsentence word that makes the statement true or false is the word, *safe*. A pragmatically unlicensed statement would be, "Vitamins and protein <u>aren't</u> very bad for your health." The way the statement is worded is like vitamins and proteins might be bad for your health. So our brains process statements based on even how the statement is structured. During the study, there was greater brain activity during the midsentence words and the brain processed the statement as false.

Certain neurochemicals contributed to stress management are prevented from being produced due to negative words. Stress producing hormones flood our system and the brain specifically the amygdala increases activity. In result, the neurotransmitters and hormones interrupt the logic and reasoning processes in the brain which in turn inhibit normal functionality.

THE ENEMY THAT IS
LURKING BEHIND

The Word of God reveals the adversary and his intent in 1 Peter 5:8 KJV: "Be sober, be vigilant; because your adversary, the devil, as a roaring lion, walketh about, seeking whom he may devour." As mentioned earlier, the enemy is very cunning and sneaky, he will use "I" statements in your thoughts so you think it is you saying it. You know, the "I" statements or the "I'm" statements. "I'm not attractive." "I'm not good enough." "I'm not smart." "I'm broke." These types of statements that we speak out of our mouths produces a seed in us, in our family, in our lives, and our atmosphere.

You may not see the effect of these words right now, but in your future, or maybe in the generation to come, it will produce a harvest. Everything that we speak is a seed. You, or someone around you, plants a negative seed and as you continue to feed it with more negativity, it will reap a full-grown harvest. Good news is that we don't have to accept all of the thoughts that come into our minds, and we don't have to say all of the thoughts that we hear internally. We can treat these types of thoughts just like we do the junk mail that we receive in the mailbox and toss them out.

When a thought comes, recognize it, and instead of speaking that thought out as one of the "I" or "I'm" statements, replace it with God's thoughts, and God's words by using the scripture to combat it. Using Jesus as the template as we walk out our lives, we can see in Luke 4 that Jesus was tempted for forty days by the devil. "And Jesus being full of the Holy Ghost returned from Jordan, and was led by the Spirit into the wilderness, being forty days tempted of the devil. And in those days he did eat nothing: and when they were ended, he afterward hungered. And the devil said unto him, 'If thou be the Son of God, command this stone that it be made bread.' And Jesus answered him, saying, 'It is written, that man shall not live by bread alone, but by every word of God'" (Luke 4:1–4 KJV). We can see that when the enemy comes with a thought, we are to use the Word of God in its true intent as the Sword to rip apart any negative statement, any words that's trying to bring confusion, strife, division. Any negative "I" or "I'm" statement that is contrary to the word of God!

The enemy uses people as vessels to speak curses and negativity in your life. The words are seeds and will produce death in you and in your situation. One would say, "Well, how would you know someone is speaking a curse over me, if they are not around?" That's why it's important to have a personal relationship with God. As your relationship grows, the Holy Spirit will reveal to you. The Holy Spirit knows all and sees all and as you develop a relationship with Him, you will become more sensitive in the spirit to see and to know these things. Your discernment may not be on that level just yet, and that's okay, but we have the power to speak and to call those things as though they already exist by using the Word of God and praying and covering ourselves and families from every negative seed sown.

HOW DO I START THIS JOURNEY OF SPEAKING LIFE?

You may have been speaking things contrary to the word of God all of your life, the good news is there is hope! Making even the smallest changes of what we say out of our mouths can make a huge impact in our lives and in the lives of those around us. Now that you have the revelation, you now have the power to make a change. As you pray and ask the Holy Spirit to help point out when you are speaking anything contrary to the word of God, and as you continue to speak life, watch how everything around you changes.

Saying this prayer will get you on track to start speaking the word of God to change your life! But before saying this prayer, and you have not been born again, the Lord is calling you to Him. He's saying come to me, "For I have come to give you life and give it more abundantly." God wants you to first confess your sins, and ask Him to forgive you of your sins. Confess that Jesus is Lord and that He died and rose again to reconcile you back to God. Believe and accept that He is the living God. You can say this simple prayer today:

> *Dear Heavenly Father, your word says that it shall come to pass, that whosoever shall call on the name of the Lord shall be saved (Acts 2:21 KJV). Today, I call on you Lord. I ask Jesus to come into my heart and to be Lord over my life! I confess that*

Jesus is Lord, and I believe in my heart that God raised Him from the dead. I thank You for saving me! Holy Spirit have your way in and through me in the mighty name of Jesus! I ask to be filled with the Holy Spirit. Holy Spirit, rise up in me. You have full course in me, and free reign in the mighty name of Jesus!

If you have prayed this prayer, congratulations! You are now a born-again believer engrafted into the Kingdom of God. It's imperative in your walk in life to stay connected to other believers to help you as you grow. Reach out to Windee Dawn Ministries INT for more information on staying connected to a ministry even if it's just for prayer: *www.windeedawnministriesint.com.*

* * * * *

Dear Heavenly Father, I come to you just as I am. Father, I repent if I have done anything knowingly or unknowingly and I ask you for your forgiveness. I humble myself before you; I seek You Lord, and turn from my wicked ways. Any negative seed sown from my mouth or anyone speaking anything contrary to your word Father, I cancel, revoke, and condemn it in the mighty name of Jesus! I bring every negative word spoken over myself or my family's lives to a naught right now in the name of Jesus! Any word spoken out of fear, anger, ill will, jealousy, bitterness, rage, anyone with a spirit of murder, may the power break now in the mighty name of Jesus! All false prophecies, any spells, hexes, incantations, vexes, potions, curses, magic, and witchcraft break now in the mighty name of Jesus! I close all doorways, gates, and windows from any curse by the power of the Holy Spirit. Any soul tie associated with a negative seed sown or curse, be broken now in the mighty name of Jesus. Flames of fire consume and engulf every negative seed, every negative word, and disintegrate it in Jesus mighty name! Remind me, Holy Spirit to speak and to meditate on those things that are just, lovely, pure, and of a good report. Cover me with your blood. Continue to give me revelation, understanding, and insight of your Word. Grant unto me discernment and break the yoke of bondage, depression, and oppression up off of my life. I take upon your yoke, for your yokes are easy and they are light. May only the Word of God that is living and powerful, sharper than any two-edged sword, piercing even to the division of soul and spirit, and of joints and marrow, and is a discerner of the thoughts and intents of the heart may remain! As I meditate on these scriptures and speak them out, may my situation change in the mighty name of Jesus!

Congratulations! You have made the first step in changing your life and situation around for the better! Don't beat yourself up if you speak negativity, but I guarantee you, you will be more conscious of what you are saying because of the Holy Spirit that lives within you. As you meditate and speak the scriptures, make them personal and make them your own. An example of making the scriptures personal and making them your own would be taking scripture Psalm 1:3 KJV that says, "And he shall be like a tree planted by the rivers of water, that bringeth forth his fruit in his season; his leaf also shall not wither; and whatsoever he doeth shall prosper." Make the scripture personal to see the changes in your life by saying, "I shall be like a tree planted by the rivers of water, that bringeth forth fruit in its season, whose leaf also shall not wither; and whatsoever I doeth I shall prosper."

With you doing that, do you know what you are doing with speaking the scripture in that way? Let's break down the scripture in the statement. "I shall be like a tree planted by the rivers of water." Trees are pretty sturdy, and being planted by the rivers of water means you will never run dry! You will never be depleted! "That bringeth forth his fruit in his season." That means that you will always be producing at the right time, there will be no stagnation or delay. "His leaf also shall not wither." You won't wither away and everything that you put your hand to won't wither away, whether that be a business, a project, a ministry, your finances! "Whatever you do you shall prosper." In every area of your life you shall be prosperous! Prosperous in relationships, marriage, family, career, business, ministry, in whatever you do! Now that's good news!

Provided on the next pages in this book are different life topics that you might be going through, or know of someone that is going through. Use the scriptures attached to the topics to make the scriptures come alive in your life. You can also use the scriptures as a ministering tool with someone you know that is going through a situation. All scriptures provided are in King James Version, however use a translation that is comfortable for you to understand.

I have a challenge for you. For the next twenty-one days, ask the Holy Spirit to help you bring to your attention every time you say or think a negative thought. When you become aware of it, counteract it with saying something positive. Say the declarations provided and begin to ask the Holy Spirit what negative thoughts or statements do you say and use the life topics section to study those scriptures and speak them out and make them personable to you. Remember consistency brings forth the change!

I decree and declare that I speak life.

May the words of my mouth and the meditation of my heart be pleasing in your sight, Father.

I decree and declare I am quick to listen and slow to speak.

Father, help me to guard my mouth.

I decree and declare my words are gracious and seasoned with salt.

I decree and declare that my mouth will utter wisdom and my tongue speak what is just.

Lord, help me to keep my tongue from evil and my lips from speaking lies.

I decree and declare that my tongue brings forth healing and is a tree of life.

I decree and declare that with my mouth I encourage others and build them up.

With my tongue, I will praise you, Lord.

SCRIPTURES

ABORTION

Before I formed thee in the belly I knew thee; and before thou camest forth out of the womb I sanctified thee, and I ordained thee a prophet unto the nations. (Jeremiah 1:5)

But when it pleased God, who separated me from my mother's womb, and called me by his grace. (Galatians 1:15)

Thine hands have made me and fashioned me together round about; yet thou dost destroy me. Remember, I beseech thee, that thou hast made me as the clay; and wilt thou bring me into dust again? Hast thou not poured me out as milk, and curdled me like cheese? Thou hast clothed me with skin and flesh, and hast fenced me with bones and sinews. Thou hast granted me life and favour, and thy visitation hath preserved my spirit. (Job 10:8–12)

Did not he that made me in the womb make him? and did not one fashion us in the womb? (Job 31:15)

Lo, children are a heritage of the Lord: and the fruit of the womb is his reward. (Psalm 127:3)

I call heaven and earth to record this day against you, that I have set before you life and death, blessing and cursing: therefore choose life, that both thou and thy seed may live. (Deuteronomy 30:19)

Thou shalt not kill. (Exodus 20:13)

So God created man in his own image, in the image of God created he him; male and female created he them. (Genesis 1:27)

For thou hast possessed my reins: thou hast covered me in my mother's womb. Thine eyes did see my substance, yet being unperfect; and in thy book all my members were written, which in continuance were fashioned, when as yet there was none of them. (Psalm 139:13, 16)

ABSTINENCE

Abstain from all appearance of evil. (1 Thessalonians 5:22)

For this is the will of God, even your sanctification, that ye should abstain from fornication. (1 Thessalonians 4:3)

But that we write unto them, that they abstain from pollutions of idols, and from fornication, and from things strangled, and from blood. (Acts 15:20)

Defraud ye not one the other, except it be with consent for a time, that ye may give yourselves to fasting and prayer; and come together again, that Satan tempt you not for your incontinency. (1 Corinthians 7:5)

What? know ye not that your body is the temple of the Holy Ghost which is in you, which ye have of God, and ye are not your own? For ye are bought with a price: therefore, glorify God in your body, and in your spirit, which are God's. (1 Corinthians 6:19–20)

ABUSE

A soft answer turneth away wrath: but grievous words stir up anger. (Proverbs 15:1)

To speak evil of no man, to be no brawlers, [but] gentle, shewing all meekness unto all men. (Titus 3:2)

The LORD trieth the righteous: but the wicked and him that loveth violence his soul hateth. (Psalms 11:5)

Know ye not that ye are the temple of God, and that the Spirit of God dwelleth in you? If any man defile the temple of God, him shall God destroy; for the temple of God is holy, which temple ye are. (1 Corinthians 3:16–17)

ACCEPTANCE

And the Lord was gracious unto them, and had compassion on them, and had respect unto them, because of his covenant with Abraham, Isaac, and Jacob, and would not destroy them, neither cast he them from his presence as yet. (2 Kings 13:23)

For by grace are ye saved through faith; and that not of yourselves: [it is] the gift of God. (Ephesians 2:8)

For God so loved the world, that he gave his only begotten Son, that whosoever believeth in him should not perish, but have everlasting life. (John 3:16)

We love him, because he first loved us. (1 John 4:19)

ADDICTION

There hath no temptation taken you but such as is common to man: but God is faithful, who will not suffer you to be tempted above that ye are able; but will with the temptation also make a way to escape, that ye may be able to bear it. (1 Corinthians 10:13)

Be sober, be vigilant; because your adversary the devil, as a roaring lion, walketh about, seeking whom he may devour. (1 Peter 5:8)

Blessed is the man that endureth temptation: for when he is tried, he shall receive the crown of life, which the Lord hath promised to them that love him. Let no man say when he is tempted, I am tempted of God: for God cannot be tempted with evil, neither tempteth he any man: But every man is tempted, when he is drawn away of his own lust, and enticed. Then when lust hath conceived, it bringeth forth sin: and sin, when it is finished, bringeth forth death. (James 1:12-15)

For all that is in the world, the lust of the flesh, and the lust of the eyes, and the pride of life, is not of the Father, but is of the world. (1 John 2:16)

Be not deceived: evil communications corrupt good manners. (1 Corinthians 15:33)

But the God of all grace, who hath called us unto his eternal glory by Christ Jesus, after that ye have suffered a while, make you perfect, stablish, strengthen, settle you. (1 Peter 5:10)

Submit yourselves therefore to God. Resist the devil, and he will flee from you. (James 4:7)

All things are lawful unto me, but all things are not expedient: all things are lawful for me, but I will not be brought under the power of any. (1 Corinthians 6:12)

Now the works of the flesh are manifest, which are these; Adultery, fornication, uncleanness, lasciviousness, Idolatry, witchcraft, hatred, variance, emulations, wrath, strife, seditions, heresies, envyings, murders, drunkenness, revellings, and such like: of the which I tell you before, as I have also told you in time past, that they which do such things shall not inherit the kingdom of God. (Galatians 5:19–21)

Dearly beloved, I beseech you as strangers and pilgrims, abstain from fleshly lusts, which war against the soul. (1 Peter 2:11)

Wine is a mocker, strong drink is raging: and whosoever is deceived thereby is not wise. (Proverbs 20:1)

And call upon me in the day of trouble: I will deliver thee, and thou shalt glorify me. (Psalm 50:15)

ADULTERY

But whoso committeth adultery with a woman lacketh understanding: he that doeth it destroyeth his own soul. A wound and dishonour shall he get; and his reproach shall not be wiped away. For jealousy is the rage of a man: therefore he will not spare in the day of vengeance. (Proverbs 6:32–34)

But her end is bitter as wormwood, sharp as a twoedged sword. Her feet go down to death; her steps take hold on hell. (Proverbs 5:4–5)

And the man that committeth adultery with another man's wife, even he that committeth adultery with his neighbour's wife, the adulterer and the adulteress shall surely be put to death. (Leviticus 20:10)

Know ye not that the unrighteous shall not inherit the kingdom of God? Be not deceived: neither fornicators, nor idolaters, nor adulterers, nor effeminate, nor abusers of themselves with mankind. (1 Corinthians 6:9)

Behold, I will cast her into a bed, and them that commit adultery with her into great tribulation, except they repent of their deeds. (Revelation 2:22)

ADVERSITY

But the God of all grace, who hath called us unto his eternal glory by Christ Jesus, after that ye have suffered a while, make you perfect, stablish, strengthen, settle [you]. (1 Peter 5:10)

[If] thou faint in the day of adversity, thy strength [is] small. (Proverbs 24:10)

And he said unto me, My grace is sufficient for thee: for my strength is made perfect in weakness. Most gladly therefore will I rather glory in my infirmities, that the power of Christ may rest upon me. (2 Corinthians 12:9)

And be not conformed to this world: but be ye transformed by the renewing of your mind, that ye may prove what [is] that good, and acceptable, and perfect, will of God. (Romans 12:2)

And God shall wipe away all tears from their eyes; and there shall be no more death, neither sorrow, nor crying, neither shall there be any more pain: for the former things are passed away. (Revelation 21:4)

Many [are] the afflictions of the righteous: but the LORD delivereth him out of them all. (Psalms 34:19)

Blessed [is] the man that endureth temptation: for when he is tried, he shall receive the crown of life, which the Lord hath promised to them that love him. (James 1:12)

So shalt thou find favour and good understanding in the sight of God and man. (Proverbs 3:4–5)

Beloved, think it not strange concerning the fiery trial which is to try you, as though some strange thing happened unto you: But rejoice, inasmuch as ye are partakers of Christ's sufferings; that, when his glory shall be revealed, ye may be glad also with exceeding joy. (1 Peter 4:12–13)

AGING

For which cause we faint not; but though our outward man perish, yet the inward man is renewed day by day. (2 Corinthians 4:16)

The glory of young men is their strength: and the beauty of old men is the grey head. (Proverbs 20:29)

Now also when I am old and greyheaded, O God, forsake me not; until I have shewed thy strength unto this generation, and thy power to every one that is to come. (Psalm 71:18)

The hoary head is a crown of glory, if it be found in the way of righteousness. (Proverbs 16:31)

With the ancient is wisdom; and in length of days understanding. (Job 12:12)

The righteous shall flourish like the palm tree: he shall grow like a cedar in Lebanon. Those that be planted in the house of the Lord shall flourish in the courts of our God. They shall still bring forth fruit in old age; they shall be fat and flourishing; To shew that the Lord is upright: he is my rock, and there is no unrighteousness in him. (Psalm 92:12–15)

And even to your old age I am he; and even to hoar hairs will I carry you: I have made, and I will bear; even I will carry, and will deliver you (Isaiah 46:4)

Hearken unto thy father that begat thee, and despise not thy mother when she is old. (Proverbs 23:22)

So teach us to number our days, that we may apply our hearts unto wisdom. (Psalm 90:12)

Thou shalt come to thy grave in a full age, like as a shock of corn cometh in in his season. (Job 5:26)

Ye shall walk in all the ways which the Lord your God hath commanded you, that ye may live, and that it may be well with you, and that ye may prolong your days in the land which ye shall possess. (Deuteronomy 5:33)

Honour thy father and thy mother, as the Lord thy God hath commanded thee; that thy days may be prolonged, and that it may go well with thee, in the land which the Lord thy God giveth thee. (Deuteronomy 5:16)

ANGELS

For he shall give his angels charge over thee, to keep thee in all thy ways. (Psalm 91:11)

Be not forgetful to entertain strangers: for thereby some have entertained angels unawares. (Hebrews 13:2)

Are they not all ministering spirits, sent forth to minister for them who shall be heirs of salvation? (Hebrews 1:14)

Bless the Lord, ye his angels, that excel in strength, that do his commandments, hearkening unto the voice of his word. (Psalm 103:20)

The angel of the Lord encampeth round about them that fear him, and delivereth them. (Psalm 34:7)

And the angels which kept not their first estate, but left their own habitation, he hath reserved in everlasting chains under darkness unto the judgment of the great day. (Jude 1:6)

Above it stood the seraphims: each one had six wings; with twain he covered his face, and with twain he covered his feet, and with twain he did fly. (Isaiah 6:2)

And I fell at his feet to worship him. And he said unto me, See thou do it not: I am thy fellow servant, and of thy brethren that have the testimony of Jesus: worship God: for the testimony of Jesus is the spirit of prophecy. (Revelation 19:10)

And he shall send his angels with a great sound of a trumpet, and they shall gather together his elect from the four winds, from one end of heaven to the other. (Matthew 24:31)

But Michael the archangel, when contending with the devil he disputed about the body of Moses, durst not bring against him a railing accusation, but said, The Lord rebuke thee. (Jude 1:9)

Take heed that ye despise not one of these little ones; for I say unto you, That in heaven their angels do always behold the face of my Father which is in heaven. (Matthew 18:10)

Likewise, I say unto you, there is joy in the presence of the angels of God over one sinner that repenteth. (Luke 15:10)

And the angel of the Lord spake unto Philip, saying, Arise, and go toward the south unto the way that goeth down from Jerusalem unto Gaza, which is desert. (Acts 8:26)

For by him were all things created, that are in heaven, and that are in earth, visible and invisible, whether they be thrones, or dominions, or principalities, or powers: all things were created by him, and for him. (Colossians 1:16)

Behold, I send an Angel before thee, to keep thee in the way, and to bring thee into the place which I have prepared. (Exodus 23:20)

My God hath sent his angel, and hath shut the lions' mouths, that they have not hurt me: forasmuch as before him innocency was found in me; and also before thee, O king, have I done no hurt. (Daniel 6:22)

Thinkest thou that I cannot now pray to my Father, and he shall presently give me more than twelve legions of angels? (Matthew 26:53)

And Elisha prayed, and said, Lord, I pray thee, open his eyes, that he may see. And the Lord opened the eyes of the young man; and he saw: and, behold, the mountain was full of horses and chariots of fire round about Elisha. (2 Kings 6:17)

ANGER

Be ye angry, and sin not: let not the sun go down upon your wrath: Neither give place to the devil. (Ephesians 4:26–27)

A soft answer turneth away wrath: but grievous words stir up anger. (Proverbs 15:1)

He that is slow to wrath is of great understanding: but he that is hasty of spirit exalteth folly. (Proverbs 14:29)

And he said, That which cometh out of the man, that defileth the man. For from within, out of the heart of men, proceed evil thoughts, adulteries, fornications, murders, Thefts, covetousness, wickedness, deceit, lasciviousness, an evil eye, blasphemy, pride, foolishness: All these evil things come from within, and defile the man. (Mark 7:20-23)

A fool's wrath is presently known: but a prudent man covereth shame. (Proverbs 12:16)

A fool uttereth all his mind: but a wise man keepeth it in till afterwards. (Proverbs 29:11)

Charity suffereth long, and is kind; charity envieth not; charity vaunteth not itself, is not puffed up, Doth not behave itself unseemly, seeketh not her own, is not easily provoked, thinketh no evil. (1 Corinthians 13:4–5)

Wherefore, my beloved brethren, let every man be swift to hear, slow to speak, slow to wrath:

For the wrath of man worketh not the righteousness of God. (James 1:19–20)

Be not overcome of evil, but overcome evil with good. (Romans 12:21)

ANXIETY

Be careful for nothing; but in everything by prayer and supplication with thanksgiving let your requests be made known unto God. And the peace of God, which passeth all understanding, shall keep your hearts and minds through Christ Jesus. (Philippians 4:6–7)

Casting all your care upon him; for he careth for you. (1 Peter 5:7)

Therefore I say unto you, Take no thought for your life, what ye shall eat, or what ye shall drink; nor yet for your body, what ye shall put on. Is not the life more than meat, and the body than raiment? Behold the fowls of the air: for they sow not, neither do they reap, nor gather into barns; yet your heavenly Father feedeth them. Are ye not much better than they? Which of you by taking thought can add one cubit unto his stature? And why take ye thought for raiment? Consider the lilies of the field, how they grow; they toil not, neither do they spin: And yet I say unto you, That even Solomon in all his glory was not arrayed like one of these. Wherefore, if God so clothe the grass of the field, which to day is, and to morrow is cast into the oven, shall he not much more clothe you, O ye of little faith? Therefore take no thought, saying, What shall we eat? or, What shall we drink? or, Wherewithal shall we be clothed? (For after all these things do the Gentiles seek:) for your heavenly Father knoweth that ye have need of all these things. But seek ye first the kingdom of God, and his righteousness; and all these things shall be added unto you. Take therefore no thought for the morrow: for the morrow shall take thought for the things of itself. Sufficient unto the day is the evil thereof. (Matthew 6:25–34)

Humble yourselves therefore under the mighty hand of God, that he may exalt you in due time: Casting all your care upon him; for he careth for you. (1 Peter 5:6–7)

I can do all things through Christ which strengtheneth me. (Philippians 4:13)

Be careful for nothing; but in everything by prayer and supplication with thanksgiving let your requests be made known unto God. (Philippians 4:6)

So that we may boldly say, The Lord is my helper, and I will not fear what man shall do unto me. (Hebrews 13:6)

Peace I leave with you, my peace I give unto you: not as the world giveth, give I unto you. Let not your heart be troubled, neither let it be afraid. (John 14:27)

Have not I commanded thee? Be strong and of a good courage; be not afraid, neither be thou dismayed: for the Lord thy God is with thee whithersoever thou goest. (Joshua 1:9)

For God hath not given us the spirit of fear; but of power, and of love, and of a sound mind. (2 Timothy 1:7)

Cast thy burden upon the Lord, and he shall sustain thee: he shall never suffer the righteous to be moved. (Psalm 55:22)

Take therefore no thought for the morrow: for the morrow shall take thought for the things of itself. Sufficient unto the day is the evil thereof. (Matthew 6:34)

Heaviness in the heart of man maketh it stoop: but a good word maketh it glad. (Proverbs 12:25)

In the multitude of my thoughts within me thy comforts delight my soul. (Psalm 94:19)

If any of you lack wisdom, let him ask of God, that giveth to all men liberally, and upbraideth not; and it shall be given him. (James 1:5)

What time I am afraid, I will trust in thee. (Psalm 56:3)

And let the peace of God rule in your hearts, to the which also ye are called in one body; and be ye thankful. (Colossians 3:15)

I sought the Lord, and he heard me, and delivered me from all my fears. (Psalm 34:4)

Rest in the Lord, and wait patiently for him: fret not thyself because of him who prospereth in his way, because of the man who bringeth wicked devices to pass Cease from anger, and forsake wrath: fret not thyself in any wise to do evil For evildoers shall be cut off: but those that wait upon the Lord, they shall inherit the earth. (Psalm 37:7–9)

ASTROLOGY

And the soul that turneth after such as have familiar spirits, and after wizards, to go a whoring after them, I will even set my face against that soul, and will cut him off from among his people. (Leviticus 20:6)

Thus saith the LORD, Learn not the way of the heathen, and be not dismayed at the signs of heaven; for the heathen are dismayed at them. (Jeremiah 10:2)

Ye shall not eat [anything] with the blood: neither shall ye use enchantment, nor observe times. (Leviticus 19:26)

And I will cut off witchcrafts out of thine hand; and thou shalt have no [more] soothsayers. (Micah 5:12)

And in all matters of wisdom [and] under-standing, that the king enquired of them, he found them ten times better than all the magicians [and] astrologers that [were] in all his realm. (Daniel 1:20)

And when they shall say unto you, Seek unto them that have familiar spirits, and unto wizards that peep, and that mutter: should not a people seek unto their God? for the living to the dead? (Isaiah 8:19)

Regard not them that have familiar spirits, neither seek after wizards, to be defiled by them: I [am] the LORD your God. (Leviticus 19:31)

ATHLETES

Be careful for nothing; but in every thing by prayer and supplication with thanksgiving let your requests be made known unto God. And the peace of God, which passeth all understanding, shall keep your hearts and minds through Christ Jesus. (Philippians 4:6–7)

Only fear the Lord, and serve him in truth with all your heart: for consider how great things he hath done for you. (1 Samuel 12:24)

Let nothing be done through strife or vainglory; but in lowliness of mind let each esteem other better than themselves. (Philippians 2:3)

Have not I commanded thee? Be strong and of a good courage; be not afraid, neither be thou dismayed: for the Lord thy God is with thee whithersoever thou goest. (Joshua 1:9)

As for me, behold, I am in your hand: do with me as seemeth good and meet unto you. (Jeremiah 26:14)

Let your speech be always with grace, seasoned with salt, that ye may know how ye ought to answer every man. (Colossians 4:6)

BAPTISM

Then Peter said unto them, Repent, and be baptized every one of you in the name of Jesus Christ for the remission of sins, and ye shall receive the gift of the Holy Ghost. (Acts 2:38)

The like figure whereunto [even] baptism doth also now save us (not the putting away of the filth of the flesh, but the answer of a good conscience toward God) by the resurrection of Jesus Christ. (1 Peter 3:21)

He that believeth and is baptized shall be saved; but he that believeth not shall be damned. (Mark 16:16)

And now why tarriest thou? arise, and be baptized, and wash away thy sins, calling on the name of the Lord. (Acts 22:16)

Jesus answered, Verily, verily, I say unto thee, Except a man be born of water and [of] the Spirit, he cannot enter into the kingdom of God. (John 3:5)

Therefore we are buried with him by baptism into death: that like as Christ was raised up from the dead by the glory of the Father, even so we also should walk in newness of life. (Romans 6:4)

I indeed baptize you with water unto repentance: but he that cometh after me is mightier than I, whose shoes I am not worthy to bear: he shall baptize you with the Holy Ghost, and [with] fire. (Matthew 3:11)

For as many of you as have been baptized into Christ have put on Christ. (Galatians 3:27)

Go ye therefore, and teach all nations, baptizing them in the name of the Father, and of the Son, and of the Holy Ghost. (Matthew 28:19)

BEAUTY

Thou art all fair, my love; there is no spot in thee. (Song of Solomon 4:7)

Favour is deceitful, and beauty is vain: but a woman that feareth the Lord, she shall be praised. (Proverbs 31:30)

So shall the king greatly desire thy beauty: for he is thy Lord; and worship thou him. (Psalm 45:11)

Lust not after her beauty in thine heart; neither let her take thee with her eyelids. (Proverbs 6:25)

Behold, thou art fair, my love; behold, thou art fair; thou hast doves' eyes. (Song of Solomon 1:15)

For which cause we faint not; but though our outward man perish, yet the inward man is renewed day by day. (2 Corinthians 4:16)

For how great is his goodness, and how great is his beauty! corn shall make the young men cheerful, and new wine the maids. (Zechariah 9:17)

Thou shalt also be a crown of glory in the hand of the Lord, and a royal diadem in the hand of thy God. (Isaiah 62:3)

For we are his workmanship, created in Christ Jesus unto good works, which God hath before ordained that we should walk in them. (Ephesians 2:10)

As the lily among thorns, so is my love among the daughters. (Solomon 2:2)

BEFORE SURGERY

Fear thou not; for I [am] with thee: be not dismayed; for I [am] thy God: I will strengthen thee; yea, I will help thee; yea, I will uphold thee with the right hand of my righteousness. (Isaiah 41:10)

Be strong and of a good courage, fear not, nor be afraid of them: for the LORD thy God, he [it is] that doth go with thee; he will not fail thee, nor forsake thee. (Deuteronomy 31:6)

What time I am afraid, I will trust in thee. (Psalms 56:3)

I can do all things through Christ which strengtheneth me. (Philippians 4:13)

BETRAYAL

And then shall many be offended, and shall betray one another, and shall hate one another. (Matthew 24:10)

Yea, mine own familiar friend, in whom I trusted, which did eat of my bread, hath lifted up his heel against me. (Psalm 41:9)

And when ye stand praying, forgive, if ye have ought against any: that your Father also which is in heaven may forgive you your trespasses. (Mark 11:25)

And I will bless them that bless thee, and curse him that curseth thee: and in thee shall all families of the earth be blessed. (Genesis 12:3)

And she said unto him, How canst thou say, I love thee, when thine heart is not with me? thou hast mocked me these three times, and hast not told me wherein thy great strength lieth. (Judges 16:15)

Debate thy cause with thy neighbour himself; and discover not a secret to another: Lest he that heareth it put thee to shame, and thine infamy turn not away. (Proverbs 25:9–10)

BIRTHDAY

The Lord bless thee, and keep thee: The Lord make his face shine upon thee, and be gracious unto thee: The Lord lift up his countenance upon thee, and give thee peace. (Numbers 6:24–26)

For by me thy days shall be multiplied, and the years of thy life shall be increased. (Proverbs 9:11)

Every good gift and every perfect gift is from above, and cometh down from the Father of lights, with whom is no variableness, neither shadow of turning. (James 1:17)

This is the day which the Lord hath made; we will rejoice and be glad in. (Psalm 118:24)

Thou crownest the year with thy goodness; and thy paths drop fatness. (Psalm 65:11)

For I know the thoughts that I think toward you, saith the Lord, thoughts of peace, and not of evil, to give you an expected end. (Jeremiah 29:11)

BITTERNESS

A soft answer turneth away wrath: but grievous words stir up anger. (Proverbs 15:1)

Let all bitterness, and wrath, and anger, and clamour, and evil speaking, be put away from you, with all malice. (Ephesians 4:31)

Say not thou, I will recompense evil; [but] wait on the LORD, and he shall save thee. (Proverbs 20:22)

Hatred stirreth up strifes: but love covereth all sins. (Proverbs 10:12)

Be ye angry, and sin not: let not the sun go down upon your wrath. (Ephesians 4:26)

If any man among you seem to be religious, and bridleth not his tongue, but deceiveth his own heart, this man's religion [is] vain. (James 1:26)

And be not conformed to this world: but be ye transformed by the renewing of your mind, that ye may prove what [is] that good, and acceptable, and perfect, will of God. (Romans 12:2)

And when ye stand praying, forgive, if ye have ought against any: that your Father also which is in heaven may forgive you your trespasses. (Mark 11:25)

For I perceive that thou art in the gall of bitterness, and [in] the bond of iniquity. (Acts 8:23)

BREAKUPS

The eyes of the Lord are upon the righteous, and his ears are open unto their cry. (Psalm 34:15)

My flesh and my heart faileth: but God is the strength of my heart, and my portion for ever. (Psalm 73:26)

And God shall wipe away all tears from their eyes; and there shall be no more death, neither sorrow, nor crying, neither shall there be any more pain: for the former things are passed away. (Revelation 21:4)

He healeth the broken in heart, and bindeth up their wounds. (Psalm 147:3)

Humble yourselves therefore under the mighty hand of God, that he may exalt you in due time: Casting all your care upon him; for he careth for you. (1 Peter 5:6–7)

Delight thyself also in the Lord: and he shall give thee the desires of thine heart. Commit thy way unto the Lord; trust also in him; and he shall bring it to pass. (Psalm 37:4–5)

And we know that all things work together for good to them that love God, to them who are the called according to his purpose. (Romans 8:28)

Finally, brethren, whatsoever things are true, whatsoever things are honest, whatsoever things are just, whatsoever things are pure, whatsoever things are lovely, whatsoever things are of good report; if there be any virtue, and if there be any praise, think on these things. (Philippians 4:8)

In every thing give thanks: for this is the will of God in Christ Jesus concerning you. (1 Thessalonians 5:18)

Let all bitterness, and wrath, and anger, and clamour, and evil speaking, be put away from you, with all malice: And be ye kind one to another, tenderhearted, forgiving one another, even as God for Christ's sake hath forgiven you. (Ephesians 4:31–32)

But they that wait upon the Lord shall renew their strength; they shall mount up with wings as eagles; they shall run, and not be weary; and they shall walk, and not faint. (Isaiah 40:31)

But love ye your enemies, and do good, and lend, hoping for nothing again; and your reward shall be great, and ye shall be the children of the Highest: for he is kind unto the unthankful and to the evil. (Luke 6:35–36)

But seek ye first the kingdom of God, and his righteousness; and all these things shall be added unto you. (Matthew 6:33)

For I know the thoughts that I think toward you, saith the Lord, thoughts of peace, and not of evil, to give you an expected end. (Jeremiah 29:11)

He hath made every thing beautiful in his time: also he hath set the world in their heart, so that no man can find out the work that God maketh from the beginning to the end. (Ecclesiastes 3:11)

Be still, and know that I am God: I will be exalted among the heathen, I will be exalted in the earth. (Psalm 46:10)

Come unto me, all ye that labour and are heavy laden, and I will give you rest. Take my yoke upon you, and learn of me; for I am meek and lowly in heart: and ye shall find rest unto your souls. For my yoke is easy, and my burden is light. (Matthew 11:28–30)

BROKEN HEART

The Lord is nigh unto them that are of a broken heart; and saveth such as be of a contrite spirit. (Psalm 34:18)

The Lord doth build up Jerusalem: he gathereth together the outcasts of Israel. He healeth the broken in heart, and bindeth up their wounds. He telleth the number of the stars; he calleth them all by their names. Great is our Lord, and of great power: his understanding is infinite. The Lord lifteth up the meek: he casteth the wicked down to the ground. (Psalm 147:2–6)

But now thus saith the Lord that created thee, O Jacob, and he that formed thee, O Israel, Fear not: for I have redeemed thee, I have called thee by thy name; thou art mine. (Isaiah 43:1)

And yet I am not alone, because the Father is with me. (John 16:32)

For I reckon that the sufferings of this present time are not worthy to be compared with the glory which shall be revealed in us. (Romans 8:18)

Rejoice not against me, O mine enemy: when I fall, I shall arise; when I sit in darkness, the Lord shall be a light unto me. (Micah 7:8)

BULLYING

For with what judgment ye judge, ye shall be judged: and with what measure ye mete, it shall be measured to you again. (Matthew 7:2)

Therefore all things whatsoever ye would that men should do to you, do ye even so to them: for this is the law and the prophets. (Matthew 7:12)

For the terrible one is brought to nought, and the scorner is consumed, and all that watch for iniquity are cut off. (Isaiah 29:20)

But I say unto you, That whosoever is angry with his brother without a cause shall be in danger of the judgment: and whosoever shall say to his brother, Raca, shall be in danger of the council: but whosoever shall say, Thou fool, shall be in danger of hell fire. (Matthew 5:22)

Let nothing be done through strife or vainglory; but in lowliness of mind let each esteem other better than themselves. (Philippians 2:3)

Blessed are they which are persecuted for righteousness' sake: for theirs is the kingdom of heaven. (Matthew 5:10)

Blessed are ye, when men shall revile you, and persecute you, and shall say all manner of evil against you falsely, for my sake. (Matthew 5:11)

Therefore I take pleasure in infirmities, in reproaches, in necessities, in persecutions, in distresses for Christ's sake: for when I am weak, then am I strong. (2 Corinthians 12:10)

But love ye your enemies, and do good, and lend, hoping for nothing again; and your reward shall be great, and ye shall be the children of the Highest: for he is kind unto the unthankful and to the evil. (Luke 6:35)

He that saith he is in the light, and hateth his brother, is in darkness even until now. (1 John 2:9)

If ye fulfil the royal law according to the scripture, Thou shalt love thy neighbour as thyself, ye do well. (James 2:8)

Thou shalt not avenge, nor bear any grudge against the children of thy people, but thou shalt love thy neighbour as thyself: I am the Lord. (Leviticus 19:18)

For God hath not given us the spirit of fear; but of power, and of love, and of a sound mind. (2 Timothy 1:7)

The Lord is my light and my salvation; whom shall I fear? the Lord is the strength of my life; of whom shall I be afraid? (Psalm 27:1)

Wherefore should I fear in the days of evil, when the iniquity of my heels shall compass me about? (Psalm 49:5)

And fear not them which kill the body, but are not able to kill the soul: but rather fear him which is able to destroy both soul and body in hell. (Matthew 10:28)

Be strong and of a good courage, fear not, nor be afraid of them: for the Lord thy God, he it is that doth go with thee; he will not fail thee, nor forsake thee. (Deuteronomy 31:6)

The Lord is my rock, and my fortress, and my deliverer; my God, my strength, in whom I will trust; my buckler, and the horn of my salvation, and my high tower. I will call upon the Lord, who is worthy to be praised: so shall I be saved from mine enemies. The sorrows of death compassed me, and the floods of ungodly men made me afraid. The sorrows of hell compassed me about: the snares of death prevented me. (Psalm 18:2–5)

For we know him that hath said, Vengeance belongeth unto me, I will recompense, saith the Lord. And again, The Lord shall judge his people. (Hebrews 10:30)

Dearly beloved, avenge not yourselves, but rather give place unto wrath: for it is written, Vengeance is mine; I will repay, saith the Lord. Therefore if thine enemy hunger, feed him; if he thirst, give him drink: for in so doing thou shalt heap coals of fire on his head. (Romans 12:19–20)

Let no corrupt communication proceed out of your mouth, but that which is good to the use of edifying, that it may minister grace unto the hearers. (Ephesians 4:29)

BUSINESS

Whatsoever thy hand findeth to do, do [it] with thy might; for [there is] no work, nor device, nor knowledge, nor wisdom, in the grave, whither thou goest. (Ecclesiastes 9:10)

But thou shalt remember the LORD thy God: for [it is] he that giveth thee power to get wealth, that he may establish his covenant which he sware unto thy fathers, as [it is] this day. (Deuteronomy 8:18)

And whatsoever ye do in word or deed, [do] all in the name of the Lord Jesus, giving thanks to God and the Father by him. (Colossians 3:17)

No man can serve two masters: for either he will hate the one, and love the other; or else he will hold to the one, and despise the other. Ye cannot serve God and mammon. (Matthew 6:24)

For the LORD thy God hath blessed thee in all the works of thy hand: he knoweth thy walking through this great wilderness: these forty years the LORD thy God [hath been] with thee; thou hast lacked nothing. (Deuteronomy 2:7)

And the LORD answered me, and said, Write the vision, and make [it] plain upon tables, that he may run that readeth it. (Habakkuk 2:2)

CHANGE

Jesus Christ the same yesterday, and to day, and for ever. (Hebrews 13:8)

For I know the thoughts that I think toward you, saith the LORD, thoughts of peace, and not of evil, to give you an expected end. (Jeremiah 29:11)

To every [thing there is] a season, and a time to every purpose under the heaven. (Ecclesiastes 3:1)

Be strong and of a good courage, fear not, nor be afraid of them: for the LORD thy God, he [it is] that doth go with thee; he will not fail thee, nor forsake thee. (Deuteronomy 31:6)

Behold, I shew you a mystery; We shall not all sleep, but we shall all be changed. (1 Corinthians 15:51)

The heart of the prudent getteth knowledge; and the ear of the wise seeketh knowledge. (Proverbs 18:15)

Therefore if any man [be] in Christ, [he is] a new creature: old things are passed away; behold, all things are become new. (2 Corinthians 5:17)

Every good gift and every perfect gift is from above, and cometh down from the Father of lights, with whom is no variableness, neither shadow of turning. (James 1:17)

Also, [that] the soul [be] without knowledge, [it is] not good; and he that hasteth with [his] feet sinneth. (Proverbs 19:2)

The Lord is not slack concerning his promise, as some men count slackness; but is longsuffering to us-ward, not willing that any should perish, but that all should come to repentance. (2 Peter 3:9)

CHEATING

Therefore to him that knoweth to do good, and doeth [it] not, to him it is sin. (James 4:17)

Lying lips [are] abomination to the LORD: but they that deal truly [are] his delight. (Proverbs 12:22)

Marriage [is] honourable in all, and the bed undefiled: but whoremongers and adulterers God will judge. (Hebrews 13:4)

Better [is] the poor that walketh in his integrity, than [he that is] perverse in his lips, and is a fool. (Proverbs 19:1)

He that walketh uprightly walketh surely: but he that perverteth his ways shall be known. (Proverbs 10:9)

[But] whoso committeth adultery with a woman lacketh understanding: he [that] doeth it destroyeth his own soul. (Proverbs 6:32)

Better [is] the poor that walketh in his uprightness, than [he that is] perverse [in his] ways, though he [be] rich. (Proverbs 28:6)

Say not thou, I will recompense evil; [but] wait on the LORD, and he shall save thee. (Proverbs 20:22)

And as ye would that men should do to you, do ye also to them likewise. (Luke 6:31)

If any man among you seem to be religious, and bridleth not his tongue, but deceiveth his own heart, this man's religion [is] vain. (James 1:26)

COMFORT

Yea, though I walk through the valley of the shadow of death, I will fear no evil: for thou [art] with me; thy rod and thy staff they comfort me. (Psalms 23:4)

Let, I pray thee, thy merciful kindness be for my comfort, according to thy word unto thy servant. (Psalms 119:76)

This [is] my comfort in my affliction: for thy word hath quickened me. (Psalms 119:50)

Shew me a token for good; that they which hate me may see [it], and be ashamed: because thou, Lord, hast holpen me, and comforted me. (Psalms 86:17)

Sing, O heavens; and be joyful, O earth; and break forth into singing, O mountains: for the Lord hath comforted his people, and will have mercy upon his afflicted. (Isaiah 49:13)

I, [even] I, [am] he that comforteth you: who [art] thou, that thou shouldest be afraid of a man [that] shall die, and of the son of man [which] shall be made [as] grass. (Isaiah 51:12)

And in that day thou shalt say, O Lord, I will praise thee: though thou wast angry with me, thine anger is turned away, and thou comfortedst me. (Isaiah 12:1)

COMMITMENT

If a man vow a vow unto the Lord, or swear an oath to bind his soul with a bond; he shall not break his word, he shall do according to all that proceedeth out of his mouth. (Numbers 30:2)

Commit thy way unto the Lord; trust also in him; and he shall bring [it] to pass. (Psalms 37:5)

Commit thy works unto the Lord, and thy thoughts shall be established. (Proverbs 16:3)

Let your heart therefore be perfect with the Lord our God, to walk in his statutes, and to keep his commandments, as at this day. (1 Kings 8:61)

And Jesus said unto him, No man, having put his hand to the plough, and looking back, is fit for the kingdom of God. (Luke 9:62)

But above all things, my brethren, swear not, neither by heaven, neither by the earth, neither by any other oath: but let your yea be yea; and [your] nay, nay; lest ye fall into condemnation. (James 5:12)

And whatsoever ye do, do [it] heartily, as to the Lord, and not unto men. (Colossians 3:23)

Into thine hand I commit my spirit: thou hast redeemed me, O LORD God of truth. (Psalms 31:5)

COMPASSION

And be ye kind one to another, tenderhearted, forgiving one another, even as God for Christ's sake hath forgiven you. (Ephesians 4:32)

And Jesus, when he came out, saw much people, and was moved with compassion toward them, because they were as sheep not having a shepherd: and he began to teach them many things. (Mark 6:34)

And it repented the LORD that he had made man on the earth, and it grieved him at his heart. (Genesis 6:6)

Bear ye one another's burdens, and so fulfil the law of Christ. (Galatians 6:2)

And Jesus went forth, and saw a great multitude, and was moved with compassion toward them, and he healed their sick. (Matthew 14:14)

Can a woman forget her sucking child, that she should not have compassion on the son of her womb? yea, they may forget, yet will I not forget thee. (Isaiah 49:15)

The Lord is not slack concerning his promise, as some men count slackness; but is longsuffering to us-ward, not willing that any should perish, but that all should come to repentance. (2 Peter 3:9)

But when he saw the multitudes, he was moved with compassion on them, because they fainted, and were scattered abroad, as sheep having no shepherd. (Matthew 9:36)

CONFIDENCE

For the LORD shall be thy confidence, and shall keep thy foot from being taken. Proverbs 3:26

Fear thou not; for I [am] with thee: be not dismayed; for I [am] thy God: I will strengthen thee; yea, I will help thee; yea, I will uphold thee with the right hand of my righteousness. (Isaiah 41:10)

Not that we are sufficient of ourselves to think any thing as of ourselves; but our sufficiency [is] of God. (2 Corinthians 3:5)

Now the God of hope fill you with all joy and peace in believing, that ye may abound in hope, through the power of the Holy Ghost. (Romans 15:13)

I can do all things through Christ which strengtheneth me. (Philippians 4:13)

So that we may boldly say, The Lord [is] my helper, and I will not fear what man shall do unto me. (Hebrews 13:6)

There is no fear in love; but perfect love casteth out fear: because fear hath torment. He that feareth is not made perfect in love. (1 John 4:18)

And whatsoever we ask, we receive of him, because we keep his commandments, and do those things that are pleasing in his sight. (1 John 3:22)

He that trusteth in his own heart is a fool: but whoso walketh wisely, he shall be delivered. (Proverbs 28:26)

Some [trust] in chariots, and some in horses: but we will remember the name of the LORD our God. (Psalms 20:7)

Charge them that are rich in this world, that they be not highminded, nor trust in uncertain riches, but in the living God, who giveth us richly all things to enjoy. (1 Timothy 6:17)

CONFUSION

For God is not [the author] of confusion, but of peace, as in all churches of the saints. (1 Corinthians 14:33)

Consider what I say; and the Lord give thee understanding in all things. (2 Timothy 2:7)

Beloved, believe not every spirit, but try the spirits whether they are of God: because many false prophets are gone out into the world. (1 John 4:1)

Howbeit when he, the Spirit of truth, is come, he will guide you into all truth: for he shall not speak of himself; but whatsoever he shall hear, [that] shall he speak: and he will shew you things to come. (John 16:13)

But they that wait upon the LORD shall renew [their] strength; they shall mount up with wings as eagles; they shall run, and not be weary; [and] they shall walk, and not faint. (Isaiah 40:31)

[We are] troubled on every side, yet not distressed; [we are] perplexed, but not in despair. (2 Corinthians 4:8)

The heart [is] deceitful above all [things], and desperately wicked: who can know it? (Jeremiah 17:9)

I [am] thy servant; give me understanding, that I may know thy testimonies. (Psalms 119:125)

COURAGE

Be strong and of a good courage, fear not, nor be afraid of them: for the LORD thy God, he [it is] that doth go with thee; he will not fail thee, nor forsake thee. (Deuteronomy 31:6)

For God hath not given us the spirit of fear; but of power, and of love, and of a sound mind. (2 Timothy 1:7)

Watch ye, stand fast in the faith, quit you like men, be strong. (1 Corinthians 16:13)

The wicked flee when no man pursueth: but the righteous are bold as a lion. (Proverbs 28:1)

Wait on the LORD: be of good courage, and he shall strengthen thine heart: wait, I say, on the LORD. (Psalms 27:14)

These things I have spoken unto you, that in me ye might have peace. In the world ye shall have tribulation: but be of good cheer; I have overcome the world. (John 16:33)

And David said to Solomon his son, Be strong and of good courage, and do [it]: fear not, nor be dismayed: for the LORD God, [even] my God, [will be] with thee; he will not fail thee, nor forsake thee, until thou hast finished all the work for the service of the house of the LORD. (1 Chronicles 28:20)

I can do all things through Christ which strengtheneth me. (Philippians 4:13)

As soon as Jesus heard the word that was spoken, he saith unto the ruler of the synagogue, Be not afraid, only believe. (Mark 5:36)

There hath no temptation taken you but such as is common to man: but God [is] faithful, who will not suffer you to be tempted above that ye are able; but will with the temptation also make a way to escape, that ye may be able to bear [it]. (1 Corinthians 10:13)

CREATIVITY

For we are his workmanship, created in Christ Jesus unto good works, which God hath before ordained that we should walk in them. (Ephesians 2:10)

And whatsoever ye do, do [it] heartily, as to the Lord, and not unto men. (Colossians 3:23)

So God created man in his [own] image, in the image of God created he him; male and female created he them. (Genesis 1:27)

Them hath he filled with wisdom of heart, to work all manner of work, of the engraver, and of the cunning workman, and of the embroiderer, in blue, and in purple, in scarlet, and in fine linen, and of the weaver, [even] of them that do any work, and of those that devise cunning work. (Exodus 35:35)

CURSING

Let no corrupt communication proceed out of your mouth, but that which is good to the use of edifying, that it may minister grace unto the hearers. (Ephesians 4:29)

Neither filthiness, nor foolish talking, nor jesting, which are not convenient: but rather giving of thanks. (Ephesians 5:4)

If any man among you seem to be religious, and bridleth not his tongue, but deceiveth his own heart, this man's religion [is] vain. (James 1:26)

But now ye also put off all these; anger, wrath, malice, blasphemy, filthy communication out of your mouth. (Colossians 3:8)

Let your speech [be] always with grace, seasoned with salt, that ye may know how ye ought to answer every man. (Colossians 4:6)

Bless them that curse you, and pray for them which despitefully use you. (Luke 6:28)

Bless them which persecute you: bless, and curse not. (Romans 12:14)

Thou shalt not take the name of the LORD thy God in vain; for the LORD will not hold him guiltless that taketh his name in vain. (Exodus 20:7)

Not that which goeth into the mouth defileth a man; but that which cometh out of the mouth, this defileth a man. (Matthew 15:11)

As he loved cursing, so let it come unto him: as he delighted not in blessing, so let it be far from him. (Psalms 109:17)

Death and life [are] in the power of the tongue: and they that love it shall eat the fruit thereof. (Proverbs 18:21)

DANCING

Let them praise his name in the dance: let them sing praises unto him with the timbrel and harp. (Psalms 149:3)

Praise him with the timbrel and dance: praise him with stringed instruments and organs. (Psalms 150:4)

Then shall the virgin rejoice in the dance, both young men and old together: for I will turn their mourning into joy, and will comfort them, and make them rejoice from their sorrow. (Jeremiah 31:13)

And David danced before the LORD with all [his] might; and David [was] girded with a linen ephod. (2 Samuel 6:14)

DATING

Be ye not unequally yoked together with unbelievers: for what fellowship hath righteousness with unrighteousness? and what communion hath light with darkness? (2 Corinthians 6:14)

And the LORD God said, [It is] not good that the man should be alone; I will make him an help meet for him. (Genesis 2:18)

Flee fornication. Every sin that a man doeth is without the body; but he that committeth fornication sinneth against his own body. (1 Corinthians 6:18)

And above all things have fervent charity among yourselves: for charity shall cover the multitude of sins. (1 Peter 4:8)

Therefore shall a man leave his father and his mother, and shall cleave unto his wife: and they shall be one flesh. (Genesis 2:24)

God [is] in the midst of her; she shall not be moved: God shall help her, [and that] right early. (Psalms 46:5)

Who can find a virtuous woman? for her price [is] far above rubies. (Proverbs 31:10)

Without counsel purposes are disappointed: but in the multitude of counsellors they are established. (Proverbs 15:22)

Meats for the belly, and the belly for meats: but God shall destroy both it and them. Now the body [is] not for fornication, but for the Lord; and the Lord for the body. (1 Corinthians 6:13)

DEATH

For if we believe that Jesus died and rose again, even so them also which sleep in Jesus will God bring with him. (1 Thessalonians 4:14)

Jesus said unto her, I am the resurrection, and the life: he that believeth in me, though he were dead, yet shall he live. (John 11:25)

But I would not have you to be ignorant, brethren, concerning them which are asleep, that ye sorrow not, even as others which have no hope. (1 Thessalonians 4:13)

And we know that all things work together for good to them that love God, to them who are the called according to [his] purpose. (Romans 8:28)

For the wages of sin [is] death; but the gift of God [is] eternal life through Jesus Christ our Lord. (Romans 6:23)

Whereas ye know not what [shall be] on the morrow. For what [is] your life? It is even a vapour, that appeareth for a little time, and then vanisheth away. (James 4:14)

For God so loved the world, that he gave his only begotten Son, that whosoever believeth in him should not perish, but have everlasting life. (John 3:16)

Yea, though I walk through the valley of the shadow of death, I will fear no evil: for thou [art] with me; thy rod and thy staff they comfort me. (Psalms 23:4)

Behold, I shew you a mystery; We shall not all sleep, but we shall all be changed. (1 Corinthians 15:51)

DEBT

The rich ruleth over the poor, and the borrower [is] servant to the lender. (Proverbs 22:7)

Owe no man any thing, but to love one another: for he that loveth another hath fulfilled the law. (Romans 13:8)

Render therefore to all their dues: tribute to whom tribute [is due]; custom to whom custom; fear to whom fear; honour to whom honour. (Romans 13:7)

The wicked borroweth, and payeth not again: but the righteous sheweth mercy, and giveth. (Psalms 37:21)

For which of you, intending to build a tower, sitteth not down first, and counteth the cost, whether he have [sufficient] to finish [it]? (Luke 14:28)

But if any provide not for his own, and specially for those of his own house, he hath denied the faith, and is worse than an infidel. (1 Timothy 5:8)

If therefore ye have not been faithful in the unrighteous mammon, who will commit to your trust the true [riches]? (Luke 16:11)

A good [man] leaveth an inheritance to his children's children: and the wealth of the sinner [is] laid up for the just. (Proverbs 13:22)

Be not thou [one] of them that strike hands, [or] of them that are sureties for debts. (Proverbs 22:26)

He that is faithful in that which is least is faithful also in much: and he that is unjust in the least is unjust also in much. (Luke 16:10)

There hath no temptation taken you but such as is common to man: but God [is] faithful, who will not suffer you to be tempted above that ye are able; but will with the temptation also make a way to escape, that ye may be able to bear [it]. (1 Corinthians 10:13)

[There is] treasure to be desired and oil in the dwelling of the wise; but a foolish man spendeth it up. (Proverbs 21:20)

DEMONS

And he said unto them, This kind can come forth by nothing, but by prayer and fasting. (Mark 9:29)

Submit yourselves therefore to God. Resist the devil, and he will flee from you. (James 4:7)

Be sober, be vigilant; because your adversary the devil, as a roaring lion, walketh about, seeking whom he may devour. (1 Peter 5:8)

Ye are of God, little children, and have overcome them: because greater is he that is in you, than he that is in the world. (1 John 4:4)

Beloved, believe not every spirit, but try the spirits whether they are of God: because many false prophets are gone out into the world. (1 John 4:1)

And be not conformed to this world: but be ye transformed by the renewing of your mind, that ye may prove what [is] that good, and acceptable, and perfect, will of God. (Romans 12:2)

DEPRESSION

Finally, brethren, whatever things are true, whatever things are noble, whatever things are just, whatever things are pure, whatever things are lovely, whatever things are of good report, if there is any virtue and if there is anything praiseworthy—meditate on these things. (Philippians 4:8)

And the Lord, He is the One who goes before you. He will be with you, He will not leave you nor forsake you; do not fear nor be dismayed. (Deuteronomy 31:8)

The righteous cry out, and the Lord hears, And delivers them out of all their troubles. (Psalm 34:17)

I waited patiently for the Lord; and He inclined to me,

and heard my cry. He also brought me up out of a horrible pit,

Out of the miry clay, and set my feet upon a rock, and established my steps.

He has put a new song in my mouth— Praise to our God;

Many will see it and fear, and will trust in the Lord. (Psalm 40:1–3)

But You, O Lord, are a shield for me, My glory and the One who lifts up my head. (Psalm 3:3)

Many sorrows shall be to the wicked; But he who trusts in the Lord, mercy shall surround him. (Psalm 32:10)

Why are you cast down, O my soul? And why are you disquieted within me? Hope in God; For I shall yet praise Him, The help of my countenance and my God. (Psalm 42:11)

Likewise you younger people, submit yourselves to your elders. Yes, all of you be submissive to one another, and be clothed with humility, for "God resists the proud, But gives grace to the humble." Therefore humble yourselves under the mighty hand of God, that He may exalt you in due time, casting all your care upon Him, for He cares for you. (1 Peter 5:5–7)

These things I have spoken to you, that in Me you may have peace. In the world you will have tribulation; but be of good cheer, I have overcome the world. (John 16:33)

For I am persuaded that neither death nor life, nor angels nor principalities nor powers, nor things present nor things to come, nor height nor depth, nor any other created thing, shall be able to separate us from the love of God which is in Christ Jesus our Lord. (Romans 8:38–39)

Blessed be the God and Father of our Lord Jesus Christ, the Father of mercies and God of all comfort, who comforts us in all our tribulation, that we may be able to comfort those who are in any trouble, with the comfort with which we ourselves are comforted by God. (2 Corinthians 1:3–4)

Beloved, do not think it strange concerning the fiery trial which is to try you, as though some strange thing happened to you; but rejoice to the extent that you partake of Christ's sufferings, that when His glory is revealed, you may also be glad with exceeding joy. (1 Peter 4:12–13)

The steps of a good man are ordered by the Lord, And He delights in his way. Though he fall, he shall not be utterly cast down; For the Lord upholds him with His hand. I have been young, and now am old; Yet I have not seen the righteous forsaken, Nor his descendants begging bread. He is ever merciful, and lends; And his descendants are blessed. Depart from evil, and do good; And dwell forevermore. For the Lord loves justice, And does not forsake His saints; They are pre-served forever, But the descendants of the wicked shall be cut off. The righteous shall inherit the land, And dwell in it forever. The mouth of the righteous speaks wisdom, And his tongue talks of justice. The law of his God is in his heart; None of his steps shall slide. The wicked watches the righteous, And seeks to slay him. The Lord will not leave him in his hand, Nor condemn him when he is judged. Wait on the Lord, And keep His way, And He shall exalt you to inherit the land; When the wicked are cut off, you shall see it. (Psalm 37:23–34)

Fear not, for I am with you; Be not dismayed, for I am your God. I will strengthen you, Yes, I will help you, I will uphold you with My righteous right hand. (Isaiah 41:10)

DESTINY

For I know the thoughts that I think toward you, saith the LORD, thoughts of peace, and not of evil, to give you an expected end. (Jeremiah 29:11)

For the vision [is] yet for an appointed time, but at the end it shall speak, and not lie: though it tarry, wait for it; because it will surely come, it will not tarry. (Habakkuk 2:3)

The LORD will perfect [that which] concerneth me: thy mercy, O LORD, [endureth] for ever: forsake not the works of thine own hands. (Psalm 138:8)

These things I have spoken unto you, that in me ye might have peace. In the world ye shall have tribulation: but be of good cheer; I have overcome the world. (John 16:33)

So shall my word be that goeth forth out of my mouth: it shall not return unto me void, but it shall accomplish that which I please, and it shall prosper [in the thing] whereto I sent it. (Isaiah 55:11)

For whom he did foreknow, he also did predestinate [to be] conformed to the image of his Son, that he might be the firstborn among many brethren. (Romans 8:29)

And we know that all things work together for good to them that love God, to them who are the called according to [his] purpose. (Romans 8:28)

Commit thy works unto the LORD, and thy thoughts shall be established. (Proverbs 16:3)

I the LORD search the heart, [I] try the reins, even to give every man according to his ways, [and] according to the fruit of his doings. (Jeremiah 17:10)

Before I formed thee in the belly I knew thee; and before thou camest forth out of the womb I sanctified thee, [and] I ordained thee a prophet unto the nations. (Jeremiah 1:5)

Hear counsel, and receive instruction, that thou mayest be wise in thy latter end. (Proverbs 19:20)

Declaring the end from the beginning, and from ancient times [the things] that are not [yet] done, saying, My counsel shall stand, and I will do all my pleasure. (Isaiah 46:10)

DIET

And God said, Behold, I have given you every herb bearing seed, which [is] upon the face of all the earth, and every tree, in the which [is] the fruit of a tree yielding seed; to you it shall be for meat. (Genesis 1:29)

Whether therefore ye eat, or drink, or whatsoever ye do, do all to the glory of God. (1 Corinthians 10:31)

Every moving thing that liveth shall be meat for you; even as the green herb have I given you all things. (Genesis 9:3)

And at the end of ten days their countenances appeared fairer and fatter in flesh than all the children which did eat the portion of the king's meat. (Daniel 1:15)

All things are lawful unto me, but all things are not expedient: all things are lawful for me, but I will not be brought under the power of any. (1 Corinthians 6:12)

[It shall be] a perpetual statute for your generations throughout all your dwellings, that ye eat neither fat nor blood. (Leviticus 3:17)

A land of wheat, and barley, and vines, and fig trees, and pomegranates; a land of oil olive, and honey. (Deuteronomy 8:8)

Take thou also unto thee wheat, and barley, and beans, and lentiles, and millet, and fitches, and put them in one vessel, and make thee bread thereof, [according] to the number of the days that thou shalt lie upon thy side, three hundred and ninety days shalt thou eat thereof. (Ezekiel 4:9)

And the Lord God commanded the man, saying, Of every tree of the garden thou mayest freely eat. (Genesis 2:16)

And they gave him a piece of a broiled fish, and of an honeycomb. (Luke 24:42)

DIRECTION

I will instruct thee and teach thee in the way which thou shalt go: I will guide thee with mine eye. (Psalm 32:8)

The steps of a [good] man are ordered by the Lord: and he delighteth in his way. (Psalm 37:23)

For I know the thoughts that I think toward you, saith the Lord, thoughts of peace, and not of evil, to give you an expected end. (Jeremiah 29:11)

And the spirit of the Lord shall rest upon him, the spirit of wisdom and understanding, the spirit of counsel and might, the spirit of knowledge and of the fear of the Lord. (Isaiah 11:2)

Call unto me, and I will answer thee, and shew thee great and mighty things, which thou knowest not. (Jeremiah 33:3)

But the LORD said unto me, Say not, I [am] a child: for thou shalt go to all that I shall send thee, and whatsoever I command thee thou shalt speak. (Jeremiah 1:7)

DISABLED

Jesus answered, Neither hath this man sinned, nor his parents: but that the works of God should be made manifest in him. (John 9:3)

And the LORD said unto him, Who hath made man's mouth? or who maketh the dumb, or deaf, or the seeing, or the blind? have not I the LORD? (Exodus 4:11)

Thou shalt not curse the deaf, nor put a stumblingblock before the blind, but shalt fear thy God: I [am] the LORD. (Leviticus 19:14)

And he said unto me, My grace is sufficient for thee: for my strength is made perfect in weakness. Most gladly therefore will I rather glory in my infirmities, that the power of Christ may rest upon me. (2 Corinthians 12:9)

But the God of all grace, who hath called us unto his eternal glory by Christ Jesus, after that ye have suffered a while, make you perfect, stablish, strengthen, settle [you]. (1 Peter 5:10)

DISCERNMENT

Beloved, believe not every spirit, but try the spirits whether they are of God: because many false prophets are gone out into the world. (1 John 4:1)

For the word of God [is] quick, and powerful, and sharper than any twoedged sword, piercing even to the dividing asunder of soul and spirit, and of the joints and marrow, and [is] a discerner of the thoughts and intents of the heart. (Hebrews 4:12)

Judge not according to the appearance, but judge righteous judgment. (John 7:24)

But the natural man receiveth not the things of the Spirit of God: for they are foolishness unto him: neither can he know [them], because they are spiritually discerned. (1 Corinthians 2:14)

If any of you lack wisdom, let him ask of God, that giveth to all [men] liberally, and upbraideth not; and it shall be given him. (James 1:5)

Give therefore thy servant an understanding heart to judge thy people, that I may discern between good and bad: for who is able to judge this thy so great a people? (1 Kings 3:9)

Behold, I send you forth as sheep in the midst of wolves: be ye therefore wise as serpents, and harmless as doves. (Matthew 10:16)

And be not conformed to this world: but be ye transformed by the renewing of your mind, that ye may prove what [is] that good, and acceptable, and perfect, will of God. (Romans 12:2)

Prove all things; hold fast that which is good. (1 Thessalonians 5:21)

DISCIPLINE

Now no chastening for the present seemeth to be joyous, but grievous: nevertheless afterward it yieldeth the peaceable fruit of righteousness unto them which are exercised thereby. (Hebrews 12:11)

Whoso loveth instruction loveth knowledge: but he that hateth reproof [is] brutish. (Proverbs 12:1)

He that spareth his rod hateth his son: but he that loveth him chasteneth him betimes. (Proverbs 13:24)

But I keep under my body, and bring [it] into subjection: lest that by any means, when I have preached to others, I myself should be a castaway. (1 Corinthians 9:27)

As many as I love, I rebuke and chasten: be zealous therefore, and repent. (Revelation 3:19)

Withhold not correction from the child: for [if] thou beatest him with the rod, he shall not die. (Proverbs 23:13)

The rod and reproof give wisdom: but a child left [to himself] bringeth his mother to shame. (Proverbs 29:15)

Love not sleep, lest thou come to poverty; open thine eyes, [and] thou shalt be satisfied with bread. (Proverbs 20:13)

For the commandment [is] a lamp; and the law [is] light; and reproofs of instruction [are] the way of life. (Proverbs 6:23)

Correct thy son, and he shall give thee rest; yea, he shall give delight unto thy soul. (Proverbs 29:17)

Foolishness [is] bound in the heart of a child; [but] the rod of correction shall drive it far from him. (Proverbs 22:15)

He that [hath] no rule over his own spirit [is like] a city [that is] broken down, [and] without walls. (Proverbs 25:28)

DISCOURAGEMENT

For I know the thoughts that I think toward you, saith the LORD, thoughts of peace, and not of evil, to give you an expected end. (Jeremiah 29:11)

And he said unto me, My grace is sufficient for thee: for my strength is made perfect in weakness. Most gladly therefore will I rather glory in my infirmities, that the power of Christ may rest upon me. (2 Corinthians 12:9)

These things I have spoken unto you, that in me ye might have peace. In the world ye shall have tribulation: but be of good cheer; I have overcome the world. (John 16:33)

Casting all your care upon him; for he careth for you. (1 Peter 5:7)

Likewise the Spirit also helpeth our infirmities: for we know not what we should pray for as we ought: but the Spirit itself maketh intercession for us with groanings which cannot be uttered. (Romans 8:26)

What shall we then say to these things? If God [be] for us, who [can be] against us? (Romans 8:31)

Now the God of hope fill you with all joy and peace in believing, that ye may abound in hope, through the power of the Holy Ghost. (Romans 15:13)

Therefore, my beloved brethren, be ye stedfast, unmoveable, always abounding in the work of the Lord, forasmuch as ye know that your labour is not in vain in the Lord. (1 Corinthians 15:58)

Submit yourselves therefore to God. Resist the devil, and he will flee from you. (James 4:7)

And the LORD, he [it is] that doth go before thee; he will be with thee, he will not fail thee, neither forsake thee: fear not, neither be dismayed. (Deuteronomy 31:8)

Wherefore seeing we also are compassed about with so great a cloud of witnesses, let us lay aside every weight, and the sin which doth so easily beset [us], and let us run with patience the race that is set before us. (Hebrews 12:1)

The thief cometh not, but for to steal, and to kill, and to destroy: I am come that they might have life, and that they might have [it] more abundantly. (John 10:10)

DIVORCE

But if the unbelieving depart, let him depart. A brother or a sister is not under bondage in such [cases]: but God hath called us to peace. (1 Corinthians 7:15)

He saith unto them, Moses because of the hardness of your hearts suffered you to put away your wives: but from the beginning it was not so. (Matthew 19:8)

The LORD shall fight for you, and ye shall hold your peace. (Exodus 14:14)

And unto the married I command, [yet] not I, but the Lord, Let not the wife depart from [her] husband. (1 Corinthians 7:10)

For the LORD, the God of Israel, saith that he hateth putting away: for [one] covereth violence with his garment, saith the LORD of hosts: therefore take heed to your spirit, that ye deal not treacherously. (Malachi 2:16)

Marriage [is] honourable in all, and the bed undefiled: but whoremongers and adulterers God will judge. (Hebrews 13:4)

DREAMS

For in the multitude of dreams and many words [there are] also [divers] vanities: but fear thou God. (Ecclesiastes 5:7)

And it shall come to pass in the last days, saith God, I will pour out of my Spirit upon all flesh: and your sons and your daughters shall prophesy, and your young men shall see visions, and your old men shall dream dreams. (Acts 2:17)

Behold, I [am] against them that prophesy false dreams, saith the LORD, and do tell them, and cause my people to err by their lies, and by their lightness; yet I sent them not, nor commanded them: therefore they shall not profit this people at all, saith the LORD. (Jeremiah 23:32)

Behold, I give unto you power to tread on serpents and scorpions, and over all the power of the enemy: and nothing shall by any means hurt you. (Luke 10:19)

EMPLOYMENT

And whatsoever ye do, do [it] heartily, as to the Lord, and not unto men. (Colossians 3:23)

But seek ye first the kingdom of God, and his righteousness; and all these things shall be added unto you. (Matthew 6:33)

For I know the thoughts that I think toward you, saith the LORD, thoughts of peace, and not of evil, to give you an expected end. (Jeremiah 29:11)

Servants, obey in all things [your] masters according to the flesh; not with eyeservice, as menpleasers; but in singleness of heart, fearing God. (Colossians 3:22)

Servants, [be] subject to [your] masters with all fear; not only to the good and gentle, but also to the froward. (1 Peter 2:18)

For the scripture saith, Thou shalt not muzzle the ox that treadeth out the corn. And, The labourer [is] worthy of his reward. (1 Timothy 5:18)

The rich ruleth over the poor, and the borrower [is] servant to the lender. (Proverbs 22:7)

And he sought God in the days of Zechariah, who had understanding in the visions of God: and as long as he sought the LORD, God made him to prosper. (2 Chronicles 26:5)

No man can serve two masters: for either he will hate the one, and love the other; or else he will hold to the one, and despise the other. Ye cannot serve God and mammon. (Matthew 6:24)

Masters, give unto [your] servants that which is just and equal; knowing that ye also have a Master in heaven. (Colossians 4:1)

And in the same house remain, eating and drinking such things as they give: for the labourer is worthy of his hire. Go not from house to house. (Luke 10:7)

[It is] vain for you to rise up early, to sit up late, to eat the bread of sorrows: [for] so he giveth his beloved sleep. (Psalm 127:2)

My brethren, be not many masters, knowing that we shall receive the greater condemnation. (James 3:1)

(For if a man know not how to rule his own house, how shall he take care of the church of God?) (1 Timothy 3:5)

But now hath God set the members every one of them in the body, as it hath pleased him. (1 Corinthians 12:18)

Seest thou a man diligent in his business? he shall stand before kings; he shall not stand before mean [men]. (Proverbs 22:29)

Let your light so shine before men, that they may see your good works, and glorify your Father which is in heaven. (Matthew 5:16)

ENDURANCE

Blessed [is] the man that endureth temptation: for when he is tried, he shall receive the crown of life, which the Lord hath promised to them that love him. (James 1:12)

Strengthened with all might, according to his glorious power, unto all patience and longsuffering with joyfulness. (Colossians 1:11)

Rejoicing in hope; patient in tribulation; continuing instant in prayer. Romans 12:12)

There hath no temptation taken you but such as is common to man: but God [is] faithful, who will not suffer you to be tempted above that ye are able; but will with the temptation also make a way to escape, that ye may be able to bear [it]. (1 Corinthians 10:13)

But let patience have [her] perfect work, that ye may be perfect and entire, wanting nothing. (James 1:4)

For whatsoever things were written aforetime were written for our learning, that we through patience and comfort of the scriptures might have hope. (Romans 15:4)

And we know that all things work together for good to them that love God, to them who are the called according to [his] purpose. (Romans 8:28)

Behold, we count them happy which endure. Ye have heard of the patience of Job, and have seen the end of the Lord; that the Lord is very pitiful, and of tender mercy. (James 5:11)

ENEMIES

Bless them which persecute you: bless, and curse not. (Romans 12:14)

Rejoice not when thine enemy falleth, and let not thine heart be glad when he stumbleth. (Proverbs 24:17)

Be strong and of a good courage, fear not, nor be afraid of them: for the LORD thy God, he [it is] that doth go with thee; he will not fail thee, nor forsake thee. (Deuteronomy 31:6)

They have prepared a net for my steps; my soul is bowed down: they have digged a pit before me, into the midst whereof they are fallen [themselves]. Selah. (Psalm 57:6)

Therefore if thine enemy hunger, feed him; if he thirst, give him drink: for in so doing thou shalt heap coals of fire on his head. (Romans 12:20)

Then said Jesus, Father, forgive them; for they know not what they do. And they parted his raiment, and cast lots. (Luke 23:34)

Though I walk in the midst of trouble, thou wilt revive me: thou shalt stretch forth thine hand against the wrath of mine enemies, and thy right hand shall save me. (Psalm 138:7)

When a man's ways please the LORD, he maketh even his enemies to be at peace with him. (Proverbs 16:7)

For mine enemies speak against me; and they that lay wait for my soul take counsel together (Psalm 71:10)

If thine enemy be hungry, give him bread to eat; and if he be thirsty, give him water to drink. (Proverbs 25:21)

ETHICS

Let integrity and uprightness preserve me; for I wait on thee. (Psalm 25:21)

Therefore thou art inexcusable, O man, whosoever thou art that judgest: for wherein thou judgest another, thou condemnest thyself; for thou that judgest doest the same things. (Romans 2:1)

FAITH

And all things, whatsoever ye shall ask in prayer, believing, ye shall receive. (Matthew 21:22)

So then faith [cometh] by hearing, and hearing by the word of God. (Romans 10:17)

But without faith [it is] impossible to please [him]: for he that cometh to God must believe that he is, and [that] he is a rewarder of them that diligently seek him. (Hebrews 11:6)

Thou believest that there is one God; thou doest well: the devils also believe, and tremble. (James 2:19)

Now faith is the substance of things hoped for, the evidence of things not seen. (Hebrews 11:1)

For with God nothing shall be impossible. (Luke 1:37)

That your faith should not stand in the wisdom of men, but in the power of God. (1 Corinthians 2:5)

For by grace are ye saved through faith; and that not of yourselves: [it is] the gift of God. (Ephesians 2:8)

(For we walk by faith, not by sight). (2 Corinthians 5:7)

Now faith is the substance of things hoped for, the evidence of things not seen. (Hebrews 11:1)

Ye see then how that by works a man is justified, and not by faith only. (James 2:24)

FAILURE

I can do all things through Christ which strengtheneth me. (Philippians 4:13)

Therefore if any man [be] in Christ, [he is] a new creature: old things are passed away; behold, all things are become new. (2 Corinthians 5:17)

If we confess our sins, he is faithful and just to forgive us [our] sins, and to cleanse us from all unrighteousness. (1 John 1:9)

For a just [man] falleth seven times, and riseth up again: but the wicked shall fall into mischief. (Proverbs 24:16)

He that covereth his sins shall not prosper: but whoso confesseth and forsaketh [them] shall have mercy. (Proverbs 28:13)

For I know the thoughts that I think toward you, saith the LORD, thoughts of peace, and not of evil, to give you an expected end. (Jeremiah 29:11)

And now why tarriest thou? arise, and be baptized, and wash away thy sins, calling on the name of the Lord. (Acts 22:16)

FAIRNESS

Open thy mouth, judge righteously, and plead the cause of the poor and needy. (Proverbs 31:9)

For God [is] not unrighteous to forget your work and labour of love, which ye have shewed toward his name, in that ye have ministered to the saints, and do minister. (Hebrews 6:10)

I returned, and saw under the sun, that the race [is] not to the swift, nor the battle to the strong, neither yet bread to the wise, nor yet riches to men of understanding, nor yet favour to men of skill; but time and chance happeneth to them all. (Ecclesiastes 9:11)

So the last shall be first, and the first last: for many be called, but few chosen. (Matthew 20:16)

Blessed [are] they that keep judgment, [and] he that doeth righteousness at all times. (Psalm 106:3)

A just weight and balance [are] the LORD's: all the weights of the bag [are] his work. (Proverbs 16:11)

Finally, [be ye] all of one mind, having compassion one of another, love as brethren, [be] pitiful, [be] courteous. (1 Peter 3:8)

There is neither Jew nor Greek, there is neither bond nor free, there is neither male nor female: for ye are all one in Christ Jesus. (Galatians 3:28)

My brethren, have not the faith of our Lord Jesus Christ, [the Lord] of glory, with respect of persons. (James 2:1)

He hath shewed thee, O man, what [is] good; and what doth the LORD require of thee, but to do justly, and to love mercy, and to walk humbly with thy God? (Micah 6:8)

For there is no respect of persons with God. (Romans 2:11)

And therefore will the LORD wait, that he may be gracious unto you, and therefore will he be exalted, that he may have mercy upon you: for the LORD [is] a God of judgment: blessed [are] all they that wait for him. (Isaiah 30:18)

FASTING

Therefore also now, saith the LORD, turn ye [even] to me with all your heart, and with fasting, and with weeping, and with mourning. (Joel 2:12)

When I wept, [and chastened] my soul with fasting, that was to my reproach. (Psalm 69:10)

That thou appear not unto men to fast, but unto thy Father which is in secret: and thy Father, which seeth in secret, shall reward thee openly. (Matthew 6:18)

I ate no pleasant bread, neither came flesh nor wine in my mouth, neither did I anoint myself at all, till three whole weeks were fulfilled. (Daniel 10:3)

But he answered and said, It is written, Man shall not live by bread alone, but by every word that proceedeth out of the mouth of God. (Matthew 4:4)

Being forty days tempted of the devil. And in those days he did eat nothing: and when they were ended, he afterward hungered. (Luke 4:2)

Defraud ye not one the other, except [it be] with consent for a time, that ye may give yourselves to fasting and prayer; and come together again, that Satan tempt you not for your incontinency. (1 Corinthians 7:5)

[Is] not this the fast that I have chosen? to loose the bands of wickedness, to undo the heavy burdens, and to let the oppressed go free, and that ye break every yoke? (Isaiah 58:6)

I fast twice in the week, I give tithes of all that I possess. (Luke 18:12)

But as for me, when they were sick, my clothing [was] sackcloth: I humbled my soul with fasting; and my prayer returned into mine own bosom. (Psalm 35:13)

So we fasted and besought our God for this: and he was intreated of us. (Ezra 8:23)

And it came to pass, when I heard these words, that I sat down and wept, and mourned [certain] days, and fasted, and prayed before the God of heaven. (Nehemiah 1:4)

FINANCE

Give, and it shall be given unto you; good measure, pressed down, and shaken together, and running over, shall men give into your bosom. For with the same measure that ye mete withal it shall be measured to you again. (Luke 6:38)

For which of you, intending to build a tower, sitteth not down first, and counteth the cost, whether he have [sufficient] to finish [it]? (Luke 14:28)

If therefore ye have not been faithful in the unrighteous mammon, who will commit to your trust the true [riches]? (Luke 16:11)

But my God shall supply all your need according to his riches in glory by Christ Jesus. (Philippians 4:19)

Every good gift and every perfect gift is from above, and cometh down from the Father of lights, with whom is no variableness, neither shadow of turning. (James 1:17)

And God [is] able to make all grace abound toward you; that ye, always having all sufficiency in all [things], may abound to every good work. (2 Corinthians 9:8)

Be thou diligent to know the state of thy flocks, [and] look well to thy herds. (Proverbs 27:23)

Every man also to whom God hath given riches and wealth, and hath given him power to eat thereof, and to take his portion, and to rejoice in his labour; this [is] the gift of God. (Ecclesiastes 5:19)

He that is faithful in that which is least is faithful also in much: and he that is unjust in the least is unjust also in much. (Luke 16:10)

FORGIVENESS

And when ye stand praying, forgive, if ye have ought against any: that your Father also which is in heaven may forgive you your trespasses. (Mark 11:25)

And be ye kind one to another, tenderhearted, forgiving one another, even as God for Christ's sake hath forgiven you. (Ephesians 4:32)

But if ye forgive not men their trespasses, neither will your Father forgive your trespasses. (Matthew 6:15)

If we confess our sins, he is faithful and just to forgive us [our] sins, and to cleanse us from all unrighteousness. (1 John 1:9)

Confess [your] faults one to another, and pray one for another, that ye may be healed. The effectual fervent prayer of a righteous man availeth much. (James 5:16)

But I say unto you which hear, Love your enemies, do good to them which hate you. (Luke 6:27)

Judge not, and ye shall not be judged: condemn not, and ye shall not be condemned: forgive, and ye shall be forgiven. (Luke 6:37)

Forbearing one another, and forgiving one another, if any man have a quarrel against any: even as Christ forgave you, so also [do] ye. (Colossians 3:13)

There hath no temptation taken you but such as is common to man: but God [is] faithful, who will not suffer you to be tempted above that ye are able; but will with the temptation also make a way to escape, that ye may be able to bear [it]. (1 Corinthians 10:13)

Hatred stirreth up strifes: but love covereth all sins. (Proverbs 10:12)

FRIENDSHIP

A man [that hath] friends must shew himself friendly: and there is a friend [that] sticketh closer than a brother. (Proverbs 18:24)

Greater love hath no man than this, that a man lay down his life for his friends. (John 15:13)

Iron sharpeneth iron; so a man sharpeneth the countenance of his friend. (Proverbs 27:17)

Wherefore comfort yourselves together, and edify one another, even as also ye do. (1 Thessalonians 5:11)

A friend loveth at all times, and a brother is born for adversity. (Proverbs 17:17)

Be not deceived: evil communications corrupt good manners. (1 Corinthians 15:33)

Ointment and perfume rejoice the heart: so [doth] the sweetness of a man's friend by hearty counsel. (Proverbs 27:9)

To him that is afflicted pity [should be shewed] from his friend; but he forsaketh the fear of the Almighty. (Job 6:14)

Faithful [are] the wounds of a friend; but the kisses of an enemy [are] deceitful. (Proverbs 27:6)

FUTURE

A man's heart deviseth his way: but the LORD directeth his steps. (Proverbs 16:9)

NUN. Thy word [is] a lamp unto my feet, and a light unto my path. (Psalm 119:105)

But seek ye first the kingdom of God, and his righteousness; and all these things shall be added unto you. (Matthew 6:33)

GOD'S WILL

Thy kingdom come. Thy will be done in earth, as [it is] in heaven. (Matthew 6:10)

Saying, Father, if thou be willing, remove this cup from me: nevertheless not my will, but thine, be done. (Luke 22:42)

For I know the thoughts that I think toward you, saith the LORD, thoughts of peace, and not of evil, to give you an expected end. (Jeremiah 29:11)

For so is the will of God, that with well doing ye may put to silence the ignorance of foolish men. (1 Peter 2:15)

In every thing give thanks: for this is the will of God in Christ Jesus concerning you. (1 Thessalonians 5:18)

And be not conformed to this world: but be ye transformed by the renewing of your mind, that ye may prove what [is] that good, and acceptable, and perfect, will of God. (Romans 12:2)

Delight thyself also in the LORD; and he shall give thee the desires of thine heart. (Psalm 37:4)

Wherefore be ye not unwise, but understanding what the will of the Lord [is]. (Ephesians 5:17)

GOSSIP

A froward man soweth strife: and a whisperer separateth chief friends. (Proverbs 16:28)

Whoso keepeth his mouth and his tongue keepeth his soul from troubles. (Proverbs 21:23)

If any man among you seem to be religious, and bridleth not his tongue, but deceiveth his own heart, this man's religion [is] vain. (James 1:26)

He that goeth about [as] a talebearer revealeth secrets: therefore meddle not with him that flattereth with his lips. (Proverbs 20:19)

But I say unto you, That every idle word that men shall speak, they shall give account thereof in the day of judgment. (Matthew 12:36)

Whoso privily slandereth his neighbour, him will I cut off: him that hath an high look and a proud heart will not I suffer. (Psalm 101:5)

To speak evil of no man, to be no brawlers, [but] gentle, shewing all meekness unto all men. (Titus 3:2)

The words of a talebearer [are] as wounds, and they go down into the innermost parts of the belly. (Proverbs 18:8)

Where no wood is, [there] the fire goeth out: so where [there is] no talebearer, the strife ceaseth. (Proverbs 26:20)

GOVERNMENT

Let every soul be subject unto the higher powers. For there is no power but of God: the powers that be are ordained of God. (Romans 13:1)

For the kingdom [is] the LORD'S: and he [is] the governor among the nations. (Psalm 22:28)

And in the days of these kings shall the God of heaven set up a kingdom, which shall never be destroyed: and the kingdom shall not be left to other people, [but] it shall break in pieces and consume all these kingdoms, and it shall stand for ever. (Daniel 2:44)

Render therefore to all their dues: tribute to whom tribute [is due]; custom to whom custom; fear to whom fear; honour to whom honour. (Romans 13:7)

GRADUATION

Grant thee according to thine own heart, and fulfil all thy counsel. (Psalm 20:4)

Let no man despise thy youth; but be thou an example of the believers, in word, in conversation, in charity, in spirit, in faith, in purity. (1 Timothy 4:12)

When thou passest through the waters, I [will be] with thee; and through the rivers, they shall not overflow thee: when thou walkest through the fire, thou shalt not be burned; neither shall the flame kindle upon thee. (Isaiah 43:2)

NUN. Thy word [is] a lamp unto my feet, and a light unto my path. (Psalm 119:105)

Be strong and of a good courage, fear not, nor be afraid of them: for the LORD thy God, he [it is] that doth go with thee; he will not fail thee, nor forsake thee. (Deuteronomy 31:6)

Study to shew thyself approved unto God, a workman that needeth not to be ashamed, rightly dividing the word of truth. (2 Timothy 2:15)

To every [thing there is] a season, and a time to every purpose under the heaven. (Ecclesiastes 3:1)

Teaching them to observe all things whatsoever I have commanded you: and, lo, I am with you alway, [even] unto the end of the world. Amen. (Matthew 28:20)

Being confident of this very thing, that he which hath begun a good work in you will perform [it] until the day of Jesus Christ. (Philippians 1:6)

I am the vine, ye [are] the branches: He that abideth in me, and I in him, the same bringeth forth much fruit: for without me ye can do nothing. (John 15:5)

And God [is] able to make all grace abound toward you; that ye, always having all sufficiency in all [things], may abound to every good work. (2 Corinthians 9:8)

Commit thy works unto the Lord, and thy thoughts shall be established. (Proverbs 16:3)

Train up a child in the way he should go: and when he is old, he will not depart from it. (Proverbs 22:6)

For where your treasure is, there will your heart be also. (Luke 12:34)

GRATITUDE

This [is] the day [which] the Lord hath made; we will rejoice and be glad in it. (Psalms 118:24)

In every thing give thanks: for this is the will of God in Christ Jesus concerning you. (1 Thessalonians 5:18)

And whatsoever ye do in word or deed, [do] all in the name of the Lord Jesus, giving thanks to God and the Father by him. (Colossians 3:17)

O give thanks unto the LORD; for [he is] good: for his mercy [endureth] for ever. (Psalm 136:1)

Cease not to give thanks for you, making mention of you in my prayers. (Ephesians 1:16)

Every good gift and every perfect gift is from above, and cometh down from the Father of lights, with whom is no variableness, neither shadow of turning. (James 1:17)

Wherefore we receiving a kingdom which cannot be moved, let us have grace, whereby we may serve God acceptably with reverence and godly fear. (Hebrews 12:28)

And let the peace of God rule in your hearts, to the which also ye are called in one body; and be ye thankful. (Colossians 3:15)

O give thanks unto the LORD, for [he is] good: for his mercy [endureth] for ever. (Psalm 107:1)

Whoso offereth praise glorifieth me: and to him that ordereth [his] conversation [aright] will I shew the salvation of God. (Psalm 50:23)

Giving thanks always for all things unto God and the Father in the name of our Lord Jesus Christ. (Ephesians 5:20)

GREED

For the love of money is the root of all evil: which while some coveted after, they have erred from the faith, and pierced themselves through with many sorrows. (1 Timothy 6:10)

But they that will be rich fall into temptation and a snare, and [into] many foolish and hurtful lusts, which drown men in destruction and perdition. (1 Timothy 6:9)

He that is of a proud heart stirreth up strife: but he that putteth his trust in the LORD shall be made fat. (Proverbs 28:25)

[Let your] conversation [be] without covetousness; [and be] content with such things as ye have: for he hath said, I will never leave thee, nor forsake thee. (Hebrews 13:5)

And he said unto them, Take heed, and beware of covetousness: for a man's life consisteth not in the abundance of the things which he possesseth. (Luke 12:15)

There is that scattereth, and yet increaseth; and [there is] that withholdeth more than is meet, but [it tendeth] to poverty. (Proverbs 11:24)

For all that [is] in the world, the lust of the flesh, and the lust of the eyes, and the pride of life, is not of the Father, but is of the world. (1 John 2:16)

No man can serve two masters: for either he will hate the one, and love the other; or else he will hold to the one, and despise the other. Ye cannot serve God and mammon. (Matthew 6:24)

He that is greedy of gain troubleth his own house; but he that hateth gifts shall live. (Proverbs 15:27)

Ye ask, and receive not, because ye ask amiss, that ye may consume [it] upon your lusts. (James 4:3)

An inheritance [may be] gotten hastily at the beginning; but the end thereof shall not be blessed. (Proverbs 20:21)

He that loveth silver shall not be satisfied with silver; nor he that loveth abundance with increase: this [is] also vanity. (Ecclesiastes 5:10)

GROWTH

But grow in grace, and [in] the knowledge of our Lord and Saviour Jesus Christ. To him [be] glory both now and for ever. Amen. (2 Peter 3:18)

Blessed [are] they which do hunger and thirst after righteousness: for they shall be filled. (Matthew 5:6)

I can do all things through Christ which strengtheneth me. (Philippians 4:13)

Being confident of this very thing, that he which hath begun a good work in you will perform [it] until the day of Jesus Christ. (Philippians 1:6)

My brethren, count it all joy when ye fall into divers temptations. (James 1:2)

Be ye followers of me, even as I also [am] of Christ. (1 Corinthians 11:1)

HATE

If a man say, I love God, and hateth his brother, he is a liar: for he that loveth not his brother whom he hath seen, how can he love God whom he hath not seen? (1 John 4:20)

Hatred stirreth up strifes: but love covereth all sins. (Proverbs 10:12)

Whosoever hateth his brother is a murderer: and ye know that no murderer hath eternal life abiding in him. (1 John 3:15)

Thou shalt not hate thy brother in thine heart: thou shalt in any wise rebuke thy neighbour, and not suffer sin upon him. (Leviticus 19:17)

Let no corrupt communication proceed out of your mouth, but that which is good to the use of edifying, that it may minister grace unto the hearers. (Ephesians 4:29)

He that saith he is in the light, and hateth his brother, is in darkness even until now. (1 John 2:9)

A soft answer turneth away wrath: but grievous words stir up anger. (Proverbs 15:1)

The fear of the LORD [is] to hate evil: pride, and arrogancy, and the evil way, and the froward mouth, do I hate. (Proverbs 8:13)

HEALTH

A merry heart doeth good [like] a medicine: but a broken spirit drieth the bones. (Proverbs 17:22)

Beloved, I wish above all things that thou mayest prosper and be in health, even as thy soul prospereth. (3 John 1:2)

Pleasant words [are as] an honeycomb, sweet to the soul, and health to the bones. (Proverbs 16:24)

If any man defile the temple of God, him shall God destroy; for the temple of God is holy, which [temple] ye are. (1 Corinthians 3:17)

And said, If thou wilt diligently hearken to the voice of the LORD thy God, and wilt do that which is right in his sight, and wilt give ear to his commandments, and keep all his statutes, I will put none of these diseases upon thee, which I have brought upon the Egyptians: for I [am] the LORD that healeth thee. (Exodus 15:26)

And ye shall serve the LORD your God, and he shall bless thy bread, and thy water; and I will take sickness away from the midst of thee. (Exodus 23:25)

Who his own self bare our sins in his own body on the tree, that we, being dead to sins, should live unto righteousness: by whose stripes ye were healed. (1 Peter 2:24)

HERITAGE

For thou, O God, hast heard my vows: thou hast given [me] the heritage of those that fear thy name. (Psalm 61:5)

Lo, children [are] an heritage of the LORD: [and] the fruit of the womb [is his] reward. (Psalm 127:3)

Thy testimonies have I taken as an heritage for ever: for they [are] the rejoicing of my heart. (Psalm 119:111)

Before I formed thee in the belly I knew thee; and before thou camest forth out of the womb I sanctified thee, [and] I ordained thee a prophet unto the nations. (Jeremiah 1:5)

HOMOSEXUALITY

Thou shalt not lie with mankind, as with womankind: it [is] abomination. (Leviticus 18:22)

If a man also lie with mankind, as he lieth with a woman, both of them have committed an abomination: they shall surely be put to death; their blood [shall be] upon them. (Leviticus 20:13)

For whoremongers, for them that defile themselves with mankind, for menstealers, for liars, for perjured persons, and if there be any other thing that is contrary to sound doctrine. (1 Timothy 1:10)

Even as Sodom and Gomorrha, and the cities about them in like manner, giving themselves over to fornication, and going after strange flesh, are set forth for an example, suffering the vengeance of eternal fire. (Jude 1:7)

Nevertheless, [to avoid] fornication, let every man have his own wife, and let every woman have her own husband. (1 Corinthians 7:2)

And likewise also the men, leaving the natural use of the woman, burned in their lust one toward another; men with men working that which is unseemly, and receiving in themselves that recompence of their error which was meet. (Romans 1:27)

Who knowing the judgment of God, that they which commit such things are worthy of death, not only do the same, but have pleasure in them that do them. (Romans 1:32)

HOPE

Rejoicing in hope; patient in tribulation; continuing instant in prayer. (Romans 12:12)

Now the God of hope fill you with all joy and peace in believing, that ye may abound in hope, through the power of the Holy Ghost. (Romans 15:13)

For I know the thoughts that I think toward you, saith the LORD, thoughts of peace, and not of evil, to give you an expected end. (Jeremiah 29:11)

Be strong and of a good courage, fear not, nor be afraid of them: for the LORD thy God, he [it is] that doth go with thee; he will not fail thee, nor forsake thee. (Deuteronomy 31:6)

But they that wait upon the LORD shall renew [their] strength; they shall mount up with wings as eagles; they shall run, and not be weary; [and] they shall walk, and not faint. (Isaiah 40:31)

Fear thou not; for I [am] with thee: be not dismayed; for I [am] thy God: I will strengthen thee; yea, I will help thee; yea, I will uphold thee with the right hand of my righteousness. (Isaiah 41:10)

And now, Lord, what wait I for? my hope [is] in thee. (Psalm 39:7)

Jesus said unto him, If thou canst believe, all things [are] possible to him that believeth. (Mark 9:23)

For we are saved by hope: but hope that is seen is not hope: for what a man seeth, why doth he yet hope for? (Romans 8:24)

And now abideth faith, hope, charity, these three; but the greatest of these [is] charity. (1 Corinthians 13:13)

For surely there is an end; and thine expectation shall not be cut off. (Proverbs 23:18)

But if we hope for that we see not, [then] do we with patience wait for [it]. (Romans 8:25)

HOSPITALITY

Be not forgetful to entertain strangers: for thereby some have entertained angels unawares. (Hebrews 13:2)

Use hospitality one to another without grudging. (1 Peter 4:9)

[But] the stranger that dwelleth with you shall be unto you as one born among you, and thou shalt love him as thyself; for ye were strangers in the land of Egypt: I [am] the LORD your God. (Leviticus 19:34)

And the barbarous people shewed us no little kindness: for they kindled a fire, and received us every one, because of the present rain, and because of the cold. (Acts 28:2)

Well reported of for good works; if she have brought up children, if she have lodged strangers, if she have washed the saints' feet, if she have relieved the afflicted, if she have diligently followed every good work. (1 Timothy 5:10)

For whosoever shall give you a cup of water to drink in my name, because ye belong to Christ, verily I say unto you, he shall not lose his reward. (Mark 9:41)

With good will doing service, as to the Lord, and not to men. (Ephesians 6:7)

A bishop then must be blameless, the husband of one wife, vigilant, sober, of good behaviour, given to hospitality, apt to teach. (1 Timothy 3:2)

That ye receive her in the Lord, as becometh saints, and that ye assist her in whatsoever business she hath need of you: for she hath been a succourer of many, and of myself also. (Romans 16:2)

HUMANITY

So God created man in his [own] image, in the image of God created he him; male and female created he them. (Genesis 1:27)

And God said, Let us make man in our image, after our likeness: and let them have dominion over the fish of the sea, and over the fowl of the air, and over the cattle, and over all the earth, and over every creeping thing that creepeth upon the earth. (Genesis 1:26)

I will praise thee; for I am fearfully [and] wonderfully made: marvellous [are] thy works; and [that] my soul knoweth right well. (Psalm 139:14)

Behold the fowls of the air: for they sow not, neither do they reap, nor gather into barns; yet your heavenly Father feedeth them. Are ye not much better than they? (Matthew 6:26)

But the fruit of the Spirit is love, joy, peace, longsuffering, gentleness, goodness, faith, meekness, temperance: against such there is no law. (Galatians 5:22–23)

And the LORD God formed man [of] the dust of the ground, and breathed into his nostrils the breath of life; and man became a living soul. (Genesis 2:7)

Jesus saith unto him, I am the way, the truth, and the life: no man cometh unto the Father, but by me. (John 14:6)

For by him were all things created, that are in heaven, and that are in earth, visible and invisible, whether [they be] thrones, or dominions, or principalities, or powers: all things were created by him, and for him. (Colossians 1:16)

And the LORD smelled a sweet savour; and the LORD said in his heart, I will not again curse the ground any more for man's sake; for the imagination of man's heart [is] evil from his youth; neither will I again smite any more every thing living, as I have done. (Genesis 8:21)

All scripture [is] given by inspiration of God, and [is] profitable for doctrine, for reproof, for correction, for instruction in righteousness. (2 Timothy 3:16)

HUMILITY

But he giveth more grace. Wherefore he saith, God resisteth the proud, but giveth grace unto the humble. (James 4:6)

For whosoever exalteth himself shall be abased; and he that humbleth himself shall be exalted. (Luke 14:11)

By humility [and] the fear of the LORD [are] riches, and honour, and life. (Proverbs 22:4)

Humble yourselves therefore under the mighty hand of God, that he may exalt you in due time. (1 Peter 5:6)

And whosoever shall exalt himself shall be abased; and he that shall humble himself shall be exalted. (Matthew 23:12)

For I say, through the grace given unto me, to every man that is among you, not to think [of himself] more highly than he ought to think; but to think soberly, according as God hath dealt to every man the measure of faith. (Romans 12:3)

Put on therefore, as the elect of God, holy and beloved, bowels of mercies, kindness, humbleness of mind, meekness, longsuffering. (Colossians 3:12)

He must increase, but I [must] decrease. (John 3:30)

[When] pride cometh, then cometh shame: but with the lowly [is] wisdom. (Proverbs 11:2)

Likewise, ye younger, submit yourselves unto the elder. Yea, all [of you] be subject one to another, and be clothed with humility: for God resisteth the proud, and giveth grace to the humble. (1 Peter 5:5)

Humble yourselves in the sight of the Lord, and he shall lift you up. (James 4:10)

With all lowliness and meekness, with longsuffering, forbearing one another in love. (Ephesians 4:2)

Thus saith the LORD, Let not the wise [man] glory in his wisdom, neither let the mighty [man] glory in his might, let not the rich [man] glory in his riches. (Jeremiah 9:23)

Boast not against the branches. But if thou boast, thou bearest not the root, but the root thee. (Romans 11:18)

IDOLATRY

Mortify therefore your members which are upon the earth; fornication, uncleanness, inordinate affection, evil concupiscence, and covetousness, which is idolatry. (Colossians 3:5)

Little children, keep yourselves from idols. Amen. (1 John 5:21)

Their sorrows shall be multiplied [that] hasten [after] another [god]: their drink offerings of blood will I not offer, nor take up their names into my lips. (Psalm 16:4)

Wherefore, my dearly beloved, flee from idolatry. (1 Corinthians 10:14)

Then shall the cities of Judah and inhabitants of Jerusalem go, and cry unto the gods unto whom they offer incense: but they shall not save them at all in the time of their trouble. (Jeremiah 11:12)

Mortify therefore your members which are upon the earth; fornication, uncleanness, inordinate affection, evil concupiscence, and covetousness, which is idolatry. (Colossians 3:5)

INFERTILITY

He maketh the barren woman to keep house, [and to be] a joyful mother of children. Praise ye the LORD. (Psalm 113:9)

Therefore I say unto you, What things soever ye desire, when ye pray, believe that ye receive [them], and ye shall have [them]. (Mark 11:24)

These things I have spoken unto you, that in me ye might have peace. In the world ye shall have tribulation: but be of good cheer; I have overcome the world. (John 16:33)

Rejoicing in hope; patient in tribulation; continuing instant in prayer. (Romans 12:12)

And thou shalt remember all the way which the LORD thy God led thee these forty years in the wilderness, to humble thee, [and] to prove thee, to know what [was] in thine heart, whether thou wouldest keep his commandments, or no. (Deuteronomy 8:2)

Through faith also Sara herself received strength to conceive seed, and was delivered of a child when she was past age, because she judged him faithful who had promised. (Hebrews 11:11)

For thou hast possessed my reins: thou hast covered me in my mother's womb. (Psalm 139:13)

Lo, children [are] an heritage of the LORD: [and] the fruit of the womb [is his] reward. (Psalm 127:3)

And Isaac intreated the LORD for his wife, because she [was] barren: and the LORD was intreated of him, and Rebekah his wife conceived. (Genesis 25:21)

He healeth the broken in heart, and bindeth up their wounds. (Psalm 147:3)

I can do all things through Christ which strengtheneth me. (Philippians 4:13)

And the LORD visited Hannah, so that she conceived, and bare three sons and two daughters. And the child Samuel grew before the LORD. (1 Samuel 2:21)

And God blessed them, and God said unto them, Be fruitful, and multiply, and replenish the earth, and subdue it: and have dominion over the fish of the sea, and over the fowl of the air, and over every living thing that moveth upon the earth. (Genesis 1:28)

There shall nothing cast their young, nor be barren, in thy land: the number of thy days I will fulfil. (Exodus 23:26)

INSECURITY

Casting all your care upon him; for he careth for you. (1 Peter 5:7)

For we dare not make ourselves of the number, or compare ourselves with some that commend themselves: but they measuring themselves by themselves, and comparing themselves among themselves, are not wise. (2 Corinthians 10:12)

Create in me a clean heart, O God; and renew a right spirit within me. (Psalm 51:10)

And ye shall know the truth, and the truth shall make you free. (John 8:32)

And such were some of you: but ye are washed, but ye are sanctified, but ye are justified in the name of the Lord Jesus, and by the Spirit of our God. (1 Corinthians 6:11)

But the Comforter, [which is] the Holy Ghost, whom the Father will send in my name, he shall teach you all things, and bring all things to your remembrance, whatsoever I have said unto you. (John 14:26)

JOY

My brethren, count it all joy when ye fall into divers temptations (James 1:2)

Now the God of hope fill you with all joy and peace in believing, that ye may abound in hope, through the power of the Holy Ghost. (Romans 15:13)

Rejoice in the Lord alway: [and] again I say, Rejoice. (Philippians 4:4)

But the fruit of the Spirit is love, joy, peace, longsuffering, gentleness, goodness, faith. (Galatians 5:22)

Hitherto have ye asked nothing in my name: ask, and ye shall receive, that your joy may be full. (John 16:24)

Whom having not seen, ye love; in whom, though now ye see [him] not, yet believing, ye rejoice with joy unspeakable and full of glory. (1 Peter 1:8)

A merry heart doeth good [like] a medicine: but a broken spirit drieth the bones. (Proverbs 17:22)

And ye now therefore have sorrow: but I will see you again, and your heart shall rejoice, and your joy no man taketh from you. (John 16:22)

For the kingdom of God is not meat and drink; but righteousness, and peace, and joy in the Holy Ghost. (Romans 14:17)

Therefore my heart is glad, and my glory rejoiceth: my flesh also shall rest in hope. (Psalm 16:9)

Rejoice evermore. (1 Thessalonians 5:16)

This [is] the day [which] the LORD hath made; we will rejoice and be glad in it. (Psalm 118:24)

JUDGING

Judge not, that ye be not judged. (Matthew 7:1)

Judge not, and ye shall not be judged: condemn not, and ye shall not be condemned: forgive, and ye shall be forgiven. (Luke 6:37)

Judge not according to the appearance, but judge righteous judgment. (John 7:24)

Thou hypocrite, first cast out the beam out of thine own eye; and then shalt thou see clearly to cast out the mote out of thy brother's eye. (Matthew 7:5)

So when they continued asking him, he lifted up himself, and said unto them, He that is without sin among you, let him first cast a stone at her. (John 8:7)

If any man among you seem to be religious, and bridleth not his tongue, but deceiveth his own heart, this man's religion [is] vain. (James 1:26)

LAZINESS

The soul of the sluggard desireth, and [hath] nothing: but the soul of the diligent shall be made fat. (Proverbs 13:4)

And whatsoever ye do, do [it] heartily, as to the Lord, and not unto men. (Colossians 3:23)

For even when we were with you, this we commanded you, that if any would not work, neither should he eat. (2 Thessalonians 3:10)

He becometh poor that dealeth [with] a slack hand: but the hand of the diligent maketh rich. (Proverbs 10:4)

He also that is slothful in his work is brother to him that is a great waster. (Proverbs 18:9)

But if any provide not for his own, and specially for those of his own house, he hath denied the faith, and is worse than an infidel. (1 Timothy 5:8)

The desire of the slothful killeth him; for his hands refuse to labour. (Proverbs 21:25)

The sluggard will not plow by reason of the cold; [therefore] shall he beg in harvest, and [have] nothing. (Proverbs 20:4)

Love not sleep, lest thou come to poverty; open thine eyes, [and] thou shalt be satisfied with bread. (Proverbs 20:13)

Slothfulness casteth into a deep sleep; and an idle soul shall suffer hunger. (Proverbs 19:15)

But Jesus answered them, My Father worketh hitherto, and I work. (John 5:17)

The hand of the diligent shall bear rule: but the slothful shall be under tribute. (Proverbs 12:24)

Go to the ant, thou sluggard; consider her ways, and be wise. (Proverbs 6:6)

LONELINESS

Fear thou not; for I [am] with thee: be not dismayed; for I [am] thy God: I will strengthen thee; yea, I will help thee; yea, I will uphold thee with the right hand of my righteousness. (Isaiah 41:10)

Casting all your care upon him; for he careth for you. (1 Peter 5:7)

Yea, though I walk through the valley of the shadow of death, I will fear no evil: for thou [art] with me; thy rod and thy staff they comfort me. (Psalm 23:4)

Be strong and of a good courage, fear not, nor be afraid of them: for the LORD thy God, he [it is] that doth go with thee; he will not fail thee, nor forsake thee. (Deuteronomy 31:6)

And the LORD God said, [It is] not good that the man should be alone; I will make him an help meet for him. (Genesis 2:18)

Teaching them to observe all things whatsoever I have commanded you: and, lo, I am with you alway, [even] unto the end of the world. Amen. (Matthew 28:20)

Lord, all my desire [is] before thee; and my groaning is not hid from thee. (Psalm 38:9)

[Let your] conversation [be] without covetousness; [and be] content with such things as ye have: for he hath said, I will never leave thee, nor forsake thee. (Hebrews 13:5)

When my father and my mother forsake me, then the LORD will take me up. (Psalm 27:10)

Trust in him at all times; [ye] people, pour out your heart before him: God [is] a refuge for us. Selah. (Psalm 62:8)

Hereby know we that we dwell in him, and he in us, because he hath given us of his Spirit. (1 John 4:13)

LOVE

Let all your things be done with charity. (1 Corinthians 16:14)

He that loveth not knoweth not God; for God is love. (1 John 4:8)

And above all these things [put on] charity, which is the bond of perfectness. (Colossians 3:14)

Greater love hath no man than this, that a man lay down his life for his friends. (John 15:13)

For God so loved the world, that he gave his only begotten Son, that whosoever believeth in him should not perish, but have everlasting life. (John 3:16)

We love him, because he first loved us. (1 John 4:19)

Beloved, let us love one another: for love is of God; and every one that loveth is born of God, and knoweth God. (1 John 4:7)

And above all things have fervent charity among yourselves: for charity shall cover the multitude of sins. (1 Peter 4:8)

If ye love me, keep my commandments. (John 14:15)

There is no fear in love; but perfect love casteth out fear: because fear hath torment. He that feareth is not made perfect in love. (1 John 4:18)

LUST

But I say unto you, That whosoever looketh on a woman to lust after her hath committed adultery with her already in his heart. (Matthew 5:28)

[This] I say then, Walk in the Spirit, and ye shall not fulfil the lust of the flesh. (Galatians 5:16)

Flee fornication. Every sin that a man doeth is without the body; but he that committeth fornication sinneth against his own body. (1 Corinthians 6:18)

For all that [is] in the world, the lust of the flesh, and the lust of the eyes, and the pride of life, is not of the Father, but is of the world. (1 John 2:16)

Meats for the belly, and the belly for meats: but God shall destroy both it and them. Now the body [is] not for fornication, but for the Lord; and the Lord for the body. (1 Corinthians 6:13)

Dearly beloved, I beseech [you] as strangers and pilgrims, abstain from fleshly lusts, which war against the soul. (1 Peter 2:11)

For to be carnally minded [is] death; but to be spiritually minded [is] life and peace. (Romans 8:6)

I made a covenant with mine eyes; why then should I think upon a maid? (Job 31:1)

Marriage [is] honourable in all, and the bed undefiled: but whoremongers and adulterers God will judge. (Hebrews 13:4)

LYING

A false witness shall not be unpunished, and [he that] speaketh lies shall perish. (Proverbs 19:9)

Lying lips [are] abomination to the LORD: but they that deal truly [are] his delight. (Proverbs 12:22)

He that worketh deceit shall not dwell within my house: he that telleth lies shall not tarry in my sight. (Psalm 101:7)

The lip of truth shall be established for ever: but a lying tongue [is] but for a moment. (Proverbs 12:19)

He that saith, I know him, and keepeth not his commandments, is a liar, and the truth is not in him. (1 John 2:4)

Wherefore putting away lying, speak every man truth with his neighbour: for we are members one of another. (Ephesians 4:25)

Ye are of [your] father the devil, and the lusts of your father ye will do. He was a murderer from the beginning, and abode not in the truth, because there is no truth in him. When he speaketh a lie, he speaketh of his own: for he is a liar, and the father of it. (John 8:44)

Thou shalt not bear false witness against thy neighbour. (Exodus 20:16)

If we confess our sins, he is faithful and just to forgive us [our] sins, and to cleanse us from all unrighteousness. (1 John 1:9)

But the fearful, and unbelieving, and the abominable, and murderers, and whoremongers, and sorcerers, and idolaters, and all liars, shall have their part in the lake which burneth with fire and brimstone: which is the second death. (Revelation 21:8)

Be not a witness against thy neighbour without cause; and deceive [not] with thy lips. (Proverbs 24:28)

A false witness shall not be unpunished, and [he that] speaketh lies shall not escape. (Proverbs 19:5)

MASTURBATION

There hath no temptation taken you but such as is common to man: but God [is] faithful, who will not suffer you to be tempted above that ye are able; but will with the temptation also make a way to escape, that ye may be able to bear [it]. (1 Corinthians 10:13)

Flee fornication. Every sin that a man doeth is without the body; but he that committeth fornication sinneth against his own body. (1 Corinthians 6:18)

But I say unto you, That whosoever looketh on a woman to lust after her hath committed adultery with her already in his heart. (Matthew 5:28)

Mortify therefore your members which are upon the earth; fornication, uncleanness, inordinate affection, evil concupiscence, and covetousness, which is idolatry. (Colossians 3:5)

But put ye on the Lord Jesus Christ, and make not provision for the flesh, to [fulfil] the lusts [thereof]. (Romans 13:14)

Neither yield ye your members [as] instruments of unrighteousness unto sin: but yield yourselves unto God, as those that are alive from the dead, and your members [as] instruments of righteousness unto God. (Romans 6:13)

MIRACLES

By stretching forth thine hand to heal; and that signs and wonders may be done by the name of thy holy child Jesus. (Acts 4:30)

Then said Jesus unto him, Except ye see signs and wonders, ye will not believe. (John 4:48)

And his name through faith in his name hath made this man strong, whom ye see and know: yea, the faith which is by him hath given him this perfect soundness in the presence of you all. (Acts 3:16)

And these signs shall follow them that believe; In my name shall they cast out devils; they shall speak with new tongues. (Mark 16:17)

And Jesus said unto them, Because of your unbelief: for verily I say unto you, If ye have faith as a grain of mustard seed, ye shall say unto this mountain, Remove hence to yonder place; and it shall remove; and nothing shall be impossible unto you. (Matthew 17:20)

Verily, verily, I say unto you, He that believeth on me, the works that I do shall he do also; and greater [works] than these shall he do; because I go unto my Father. (John 14:12)

And God wrought special miracles by the hands of Paul. (Acts 19:11)

When Jesus heard [that], he said, This sickness is not unto death, but for the glory of God, that the Son of God might be glorified thereby. (John 11:4)

[Even him], whose coming is after the working of Satan with all power and signs and lying wonders. (2 Thessalonians 2:9)

MISCARRIAGE

For I reckon that the sufferings of this present time [are] not worthy [to be compared] with the glory which shall be revealed in us. (Romans 8:18)

There shall nothing cast their young, nor be barren, in thy land: the number of thy days I will fulfil. (Exodus 23:26)

Even so it is not the will of your Father which is in heaven, that one of these little ones should perish. (Matthew 18:14)

For I know the thoughts that I think toward you, saith the LORD, thoughts of peace, and not of evil, to give you an expected end. (Jeremiah 29:11)

He healeth the broken in heart, and bindeth up their wounds. (Psalm 147:3)

Before I formed thee in the belly I knew thee; and before thou camest forth out of the womb I sanctified thee, [and] I ordained thee a prophet unto the nations. (Jeremiah 1:5)

As thou knowest not what [is] the way of the spirit, [nor] how the bones [do grow] in the womb of her that is with child: even so thou knowest not the works of God who maketh all. (Ecclesiastes 11:5)

(For [the children] being not yet born, neither having done any good or evil, that the purpose of God according to election might stand, not of works, but of him that calleth). (Romans 9:11)

Fear thou not; for I [am] with thee: be not dismayed; for I [am] thy God: I will strengthen thee; yea, I will help thee; yea, I will uphold thee with the right hand of my righteousness. (Isaiah 41:10)

Can a woman forget her sucking child, that she should not have compassion on the son of her womb? yea, they may forget, yet will I not forget thee. (Isaiah 49:15)

Whom I have sent again: thou therefore receive him, that is, mine own bowels. (Philemon 1:12)

Thine eyes did see my substance, yet being unperfect; and in thy book all [my members] were written, [which] in continuance were fashioned, when [as yet there was] none of them. (Psalm 139:16)

And said, Naked came I out of my mother's womb, and naked shall I return thither: the LORD gave, and the LORD hath taken away; blessed be the name of the LORD. (Job 1:21)

I sought the LORD, and he heard me, and delivered me from all my fears. (Psalm 34:4)

Is any among you afflicted? let him pray. Is any merry? let him sing psalms. (James 5:13)

They shall not labour in vain, nor bring forth for trouble; for they [are] the seed of the blessed of the LORD, and their offspring with them. (Isaiah 65:23)

MONEY

[Let your] conversation [be] without covetousness; [and be] content with such things as ye have: for he hath said, I will never leave thee, nor forsake thee. (Hebrews 13:5)

For the love of money is the root of all evil: which while some coveted after, they have erred from the faith, and pierced themselves through with many sorrows. (1 Timothy 6:10)

No man can serve two masters: for either he will hate the one, and love the other; or else he will hold to the one, and despise the other. Ye cannot serve God and mammon. (Matthew 6:24)

He that loveth silver shall not be satisfied with silver; nor he that loveth abundance with increase: this [is] also vanity. (Ecclesiastes 5:10)

Wealth [gotten] by vanity shall be diminished: but he that gathereth by labour shall increase. (Proverbs 13:11)

The rich ruleth over the poor, and the borrower [is] servant to the lender. (Proverbs 22:7)

But if any provide not for his own, and specially for those of his own house, he hath denied the faith, and is worse than an infidel. (1 Timothy 5:8)

If therefore ye have not been faithful in the unrighteous mammon, who will commit to your trust the true [riches]? (Luke 16:11)

A [good] name [is] rather to be chosen than great riches, [and] loving favour rather than silver and gold. (Proverbs 22:1)

MOTIVES

Every way of a man [is] right in his own eyes: but the LORD pondereth the hearts. (Proverbs 21:2)

For do I now persuade men, or God? or do I seek to please men? for if I yet pleased men, I should not be the servant of Christ. (Galatians 1:10)

But as we were allowed of God to be put in trust with the gospel, even so we speak; not as pleasing men, but God, which trieth our hearts. (1 Thessalonians 2:4)

[Let] nothing [be done] through strife or vainglory; but in lowliness of mind let each esteem other better than themselves. (Philippians 2:3)

Take heed that ye do not your alms before men, to be seen of them: otherwise ye have no reward of your Father which is in heaven. (Matthew 6:1)

Now the end of the commandment is charity out of a pure heart, and [of] a good conscience, and [of] faith unfeigned. (1 Timothy 1:5)

But the LORD said unto Samuel, Look not on his countenance, or on the height of his stature; because I have refused him: for [the LORD seeth] not as man seeth; for man looketh on the outward appearance, but the LORD looketh on the heart. (1 Samuel 16:7)

Therefore judge nothing before the time, until the Lord come, who both will bring to light the hidden things of darkness, and will make manifest the counsels of the hearts: and then shall every man have praise of God. (1 Corinthians 4:5)

Not as Cain, [who] was of that wicked one, and slew his brother. And wherefore slew he him? Because his own works were evil, and his brother's righteous. (1 John 3:12)

All the ways of a man [are] clean in his own eyes; but the LORD weigheth the spirits. (Proverbs 16:2)

Beloved, believe not every spirit, but try the spirits whether they are of God: because many false prophets are gone out into the world. (1 John 4:1)

If thou doest well, shalt thou not be accepted? and if thou doest not well, sin lieth at the door. And unto thee [shall be] his desire, and thou shalt rule over him. (Genesis 4:7)

And whatsoever ye do in word or deed, [do] all in the name of the Lord Jesus, giving thanks to God and the Father by him. (Colossians 3:17)

MUSIC

Sing unto him, sing psalms unto him: talk ye of all his wondrous works. (Psalm 105:2)

I will sing unto the LORD as long as I live: I will sing praise to my God while I have my being. (Psalm 104:33)

Speaking to yourselves in psalms and hymns and spiritual songs, singing and making melody in your heart to the Lord. (Ephesians 5:19)

O come, let us sing unto the LORD: let us make a joyful noise to the rock of our salvation. (Psalm 95:1)

Let the word of Christ dwell in you richly in all wisdom; teaching and admonishing one another in psalms and hymns and spiritual songs, singing with grace in your hearts to the Lord. (Colossians 3:16)

Is any among you afflicted? let him pray. Is any merry? let him sing psalms. (James 5:13)

[It is] better to hear the rebuke of the wise, than for a man to hear the song of fools. (Ecclesiastes 7:5)

My lips shall greatly rejoice when I sing unto thee; and my soul, which thou hast redeemed. (Psalm 71:23)

[As] he that taketh away a garment in cold weather, [and as] vinegar upon nitre, so [is] he that singeth songs to an heavy heart. (Proverbs 25:20)

Finally, brethren, whatsoever things are true, whatsoever things [are] honest, whatsoever things [are] just, whatsoever things [are] pure, whatsoever things [are] lovely, whatsoever things [are] of good report; if [there be] any virtue, and if [there be] any praise, think on these things. (Philippians 4:8)

OBEDIENCE

If ye love me, keep my commandments. (John 14:15)

And why call ye me, Lord, Lord, and do not the things which I say? (Luke 6:46)

Know ye not, that to whom ye yield yourselves servants to obey, his servants ye are to whom ye obey; whether of sin unto death, or of obedience unto righteousness? (Romans 6:16)

Not every one that saith unto me, Lord, Lord, shall enter into the kingdom of heaven; but he that doeth the will of my Father which is in heaven. (Matthew 7:21)

But be ye doers of the word, and not hearers only, deceiving your own selves. (James 1:22)

If ye be willing and obedient, ye shall eat the good of the land. (Isaiah 1:19)

And Samuel said, Hath the LORD [as great] delight in burnt offerings and sacrifices, as in obeying the voice of the LORD? Behold, to obey [is] better than sacrifice, [and] to hearken than the fat of rams. (1 Samuel 15:22)

And we know that all things work together for good to them that love God, to them who are the called according to [his] purpose. (Romans 8:28)

Ye see then how that by works a man is justified, and not by faith only. (James 2:24)

He that hath my commandments, and keepeth them, he it is that loveth me: and he that loveth me shall be loved of my Father, and I will love him, and will manifest myself to him. (John 14:21)

Because strait [is] the gate, and narrow [is] the way, which leadeth unto life, and few there be that find it. (Matthew 7:14)

For to this end also did I write, that I might know the proof of you, whether ye be obedient in all things. (2 Corinthians 2:9)

OVERCOMING GRIEF

The LORD [is] nigh unto them that are of a broken heart; and saveth such as be of a contrite spirit. (Psalm 34:18)

And God shall wipe away all tears from their eyes; and there shall be no more death, neither sorrow, nor crying, neither shall there be any more pain: for the former things are passed away. (Revelation 21:4)

He healeth the broken in heart, and bindeth up their wounds. (Psalm 147:3)

Casting all your care upon him; for he careth for you. (1 Peter 5:7)

My flesh and my heart faileth: [but] God [is] the strength of my heart, and my portion for ever. (Psalm 73:26)

Blessed [are] they that mourn: for they shall be comforted. (Matthew 5:4)

A little while, and ye shall not see me: and again, a little while, and ye shall see me, because I go to the Father. (John 16:16)

Peace I leave with you, my peace I give unto you: not as the world giveth, give I unto you.

Let not your heart be troubled, neither let it be afraid. (John 14:27)

For God so loved the world, that he gave his only begotten Son, that whosoever believeth in him should not perish, but have everlasting life. (John 3:16)

Thou wilt keep [him] in perfect peace, [whose] mind [is] stayed [on thee]: because he trusteth in thee. (Isaiah 26:3)

But I would not have you to be ignorant, brethren, concerning them which are asleep, that ye sorrow not, even as others which have no hope. (1 Thessalonians 4:13)

Let not your heart be troubled: ye believe in God, believe also in me. (John 14:1)

PAIN

And God shall wipe away all tears from their eyes; and there shall be no more death, neither sorrow, nor crying, neither shall there be any more pain: for the former things are passed away. (Revelation 21:4)

For I reckon that the sufferings of this present time [are] not worthy [to be compared] with the glory which shall be revealed in us. (Romans 8:18)

The LORD will strengthen him upon the bed of languishing: thou wilt make all his bed in his sickness. (Psalm 41:3)

My bones are pierced in me in the night season: and my sinews take no rest. (Job 30:17)

Wherefore let them that suffer according to the will of God commit the keeping of their souls [to him] in well doing, as unto a faithful Creator. (1 Peter 4:19)

Why is my pain perpetual, and my wound incurable, [which] refuseth to be healed? wilt thou be altogether unto me as a liar, [and as] waters [that] fail? (Jeremiah 15:18)

I can do all things through Christ which strengtheneth me. (Philippians 4:13)

But his flesh upon him shall have pain, and his soul within him shall mourn. (Job 14:22)

For I know the thoughts that I think toward you, saith the LORD, thoughts of peace, and not of evil, to give you an expected end. (Jeremiah 29:11)

Beloved, think it not strange concerning the fiery trial which is to try you, as though some strange thing happened unto you. (1 Peter 4:12)

The blueness of a wound cleanseth away evil: so [do] stripes the inward parts of the belly. (Proverbs 20:30)

He is chastened also with pain upon his bed, and the multitude of his bones with strong [pain]. (Job 33:19)

PARENTING

Train up a child in the way he should go: and when he is old, he will not depart from it. (Proverbs 22:6)

And, ye fathers, provoke not your children to wrath: but bring them up in the nurture and admonition of the Lord. (Ephesians 6:4)

In all things shewing thyself a pattern of good works: in doctrine [shewing] uncorruptness, gravity, sincerity. (Titus 2:7)

Lo, children [are] an heritage of the LORD: [and] the fruit of the womb [is his] reward. (Psalm 127:3)

He that spareth his rod hateth his son: but he that loveth him chasteneth him betimes. (Proverbs 13:24)

Fathers, provoke not your children [to anger], lest they be discouraged. (Colossians 3:21)

The rod and reproof give wisdom: but a child left [to himself] bringeth his mother to shame. (Proverbs 29:15)

Correct thy son, and he shall give thee rest; yea, he shall give delight unto thy soul. (Proverbs 29:17)

Withhold not correction from the child: for [if] thou beatest him with the rod, he shall not die. (Proverbs 23:13)

Neither as being lords over [God's] heritage, but being ensamples to the flock. (1 Peter 5:3)

PEER PRESSURE

He that walketh with wise [men] shall be wise: but a companion of fools shall be destroyed. (Proverbs 13:20)

And be not conformed to this world: but be ye transformed by the renewing of your mind, that ye may prove what [is] that good, and acceptable, and perfect, will of God. (Romans 12:2)

There hath no temptation taken you but such as is common to man: but God [is] faithful, who will not suffer you to be tempted above that ye are able; but will with the temptation also make a way to escape, that ye may be able to bear [it]. (1 Corinthians 10:13)

For do I now persuade men, or God? or do I seek to please men? for if I yet pleased men, I should not be the servant of Christ. (Galatians 1:10)

My son, if sinners entice thee, consent thou not. (Proverbs 1:10)

Then Peter and the [other] apostles answered and said, We ought to obey God rather than men. (Acts 5:29)

Be not deceived: evil communications corrupt good manners. (1 Corinthians 15:33)

For what is a man profited, if he shall gain the whole world, and lose his own soul? or what shall a man give in exchange for his soul? (Matthew 16:26)

And [so] Pilate, willing to content the people, released Barabbas unto them, and delivered Jesus, when he had scourged [him], to be crucified. (Mark 15:15)

PLANS

For I know the thoughts that I think toward you, saith the LORD, thoughts of peace, and not of evil, to give you an expected end. (Jeremiah 29:11)

Commit thy works unto the LORD, and thy thoughts shall be established. (Proverbs 16:3)

A man's heart deviseth his way: but the LORD directeth his steps. (Proverbs 16:9)

But seek ye first the kingdom of God, and his righteousness; and all these things shall be added unto you. (Matthew 6:33)

Study to shew thyself approved unto God, a workman that needeth not to be ashamed, rightly dividing the word of truth. (2 Timothy 2:15)

Come unto me, all [ye] that labour and are heavy laden, and I will give you rest. (Matthew 11:28)

And the LORD answered me, and said, Write the vision, and make [it] plain upon tables, that he may run that readeth it. (Habakkuk 2:2)

PORNOGRAPHY

But I say unto you, That whosoever looketh on a woman to lust after her hath committed adultery with her already in his heart. (Matthew 5:28)

Turn away mine eyes from beholding vanity; [and] quicken thou me in thy way. (Psalm 119:37)

There hath no temptation taken you but such as is common to man: but God [is] faithful, who will not suffer you to be tempted above that ye are able; but will with the temptation also make a way to escape, that ye may be able to bear [it]. (1 Corinthians 10:13)

For all that [is] in the world, the lust of the flesh, and the lust of the eyes, and the pride of life, is not of the Father, but is of the world. (1 John 2:16)

Finally, brethren, whatsoever things are true, whatsoever things [are] honest, whatsoever things [are] just, whatsoever things [are] pure, whatsoever things [are] lovely, whatsoever things [are] of good report; if [there be] any virtue, and if [there be] any praise, think on these things. (Philippians 4:8)

Know ye not that the unrighteous shall not inherit the kingdom of God? Be not deceived: neither fornicators, nor idolaters, nor adulterers, nor effeminate, nor abusers of themselves with mankind. (1 Corinthians 6:9)

I made a covenant with mine eyes; why then should I think upon a maid? (Job 31:1)

Meats for the belly, and the belly for meats: but God shall destroy both it and them. Now the body [is] not for fornication, but for the Lord; and the Lord for the body. (1 Corinthians 6:13)

POPULARITY

For what is a man advantaged, if he gain the whole world, and lose himself, or be cast away? (Luke 9:25)

He that walketh with wise [men] shall be wise: but a companion of fools shall be destroyed. (Proverbs 13:20)

And be not conformed to this world: but be ye transformed by the renewing of your mind, that ye may prove what [is] that good, and acceptable, and perfect, will of God. (Romans 12:2)

Woe unto you, when all men shall speak well of you! for so did their fathers to the false prophets. (Luke 6:26)

The fear of man bringeth a snare: but whoso putteth his trust in the LORD shall be safe. (Proverbs 29:25)

But the LORD said unto Samuel, Look not on his countenance, or on the height of his stature; because I have refused him: for [the LORD seeth] not as man seeth; for man looketh on the outward appearance, but the LORD looketh on the heart. (1 Samuel 16:7)

Be sober, be vigilant; because your adversary the devil, as a roaring lion, walketh about, seeking whom he may devour. (1 Peter 5:8)

Ye adulterers and adulteresses, know ye not that the friendship of the world is enmity with God? whosoever therefore will be a friend of the world is the enemy of God. (James 4:4)

And all the people took notice [of it], and it pleased them: as whatsoever the king did pleased all the people. (2 Samuel 3:36)

A man's pride shall bring him low: but honour shall uphold the humble in spirit. (Proverbs 29:23)

A man [that hath] friends must shew himself friendly: and there is a friend [that] sticketh closer than a brother. (Proverbs 18:24)

And we know that all things work together for good to them that love God, to them who are the called according to [his] purpose. (Romans 8:28)

PRAYER

Be careful for nothing; but in every thing by prayer and supplication with thanksgiving let your requests be made known unto God. (Philippians 4:6)

If ye abide in me, and my words abide in you, ye shall ask what ye will, and it shall be done unto you. (John 15:7)

Therefore I say unto you, What things soever ye desire, when ye pray, believe that ye receive [them], and ye shall have [them]. (Mark 11:24)

Pray without ceasing. (1 Thessalonians 5:17)

Likewise the Spirit also helpeth our infirmities: for we know not what we should pray for as we ought: but the Spirit itself maketh intercession for us with groanings which cannot be uttered. (Romans 8:26)

But thou, when thou prayest, enter into thy closet, and when thou hast shut thy door, pray to thy Father which is in secret; and thy Father which seeth in secret shall reward thee openly. (Matthew 6:6)

But when ye pray, use not vain repetitions, as the heathen [do]: for they think that they shall be heard for their much speaking. (Matthew 6:7)

And I say unto you, Ask, and it shall be given you; seek, and ye shall find; knock, and it shall be opened unto you. (Luke 11:9)

Call unto me, and I will answer thee, and shew thee great and mighty things, which thou knowest not. (Jeremiah 33:3)

Watch and pray, that ye enter not into temptation: the spirit indeed [is] willing, but the flesh [is] weak. (Matthew 26:41)

For [there is] one God, and one mediator between God and men, the man Christ Jesus. (1 Timothy 2:5)

Confess [your] faults one to another, and pray one for another, that ye may be healed. The effectual fervent prayer of a righteous man availeth much. (James 5:16)

Praying always with all prayer and supplication in the Spirit, and watching thereunto with all perseverance and supplication for all saints. (Ephesians 6:18)

[The righteous] cry, and the LORD heareth, and delivereth them out of all their troubles. (Psalm 34:17)

And he spake a parable unto them [to this end], that men ought always to pray, and not to faint. (Luke 18:1)

PREGNANCY

Lo, children [are] an heritage of the LORD: [and] the fruit of the womb [is his] reward. (Psalm 127:3)

Before I formed thee in the belly I knew thee; and before thou camest forth out of the womb I sanctified thee, [and] I ordained thee a prophet unto the nations. (Jeremiah 1:5)

Did not he that made me in the womb make him? and did not one fashion us in the womb? (Job 31:15)

As thou knowest not what [is] the way of the spirit, [nor] how the bones [do grow] in the womb of her that is with child: even so thou knowest not the works of God who maketh all. (Ecclesiastes 11:5)

Can a woman forget her sucking child, that she should not have compassion on the son of her womb? yea, they may forget, yet will I not forget thee. (Isaiah 49:15)

For thou hast possessed my reins: thou hast covered me in my mother's womb. (Psalm 139:13)

A woman when she is in travail hath sorrow, because her hour is come: but as soon as she is delivered of the child, she remembereth no more the anguish, for joy that a man is born into the world. (John 16:21)

And the angel of the LORD said unto her, Behold, thou [art] with child, and shalt bear a son, and shalt call his name Ishmael; because the LORD hath heard thy affliction. (Genesis 16:11)

For, behold, the days are coming, in the which they shall say, Blessed [are] the barren, and the wombs that never bare, and the paps which never gave suck. (Luke 23:29)

Unto the woman he said, I will greatly multiply thy sorrow and thy conception; in sorrow thou shalt bring forth children; and thy desire [shall be] to thy husband, and he shall rule over thee. (Genesis 3:16)

I was cast upon thee from the womb: thou [art] my God from my mother's belly. (Psalm 22:10)

He maketh the barren woman to keep house, [and to be] a joyful mother of children. Praise ye the LORD. (Psalm 113:9)

And he will love thee, and bless thee, and multiply thee: he will also bless the fruit of thy womb, and the fruit of thy land, thy corn, and thy wine, and thine oil, the increase of thy kine, and the flocks of thy sheep, in the land which he sware unto thy fathers to give thee. (Deuteronomy 7:13)

Thy father and thy mother shall be glad, and she that bare thee shall rejoice. (Proverbs 23:25)

And the angel of the LORD appeared unto the woman, and said unto her, Behold now, thou

[art] barren, and bearest not: but thou shalt conceive, and bear a son. (Judges 13:3)

And Isaac intreated the LORD for his wife, because she [was] barren: and the LORD was intreated of him, and Rebekah his wife conceived. (Genesis 25:21)

Her children arise up, and call her blessed; her husband [also], and he praiseth her. (Proverbs 31:28)

And the LORD visited Hannah, so that she conceived, and bare three sons and two daughters. And the child Samuel grew before the LORD. (1 Samuel 2:21)

And thou shalt have joy and gladness; and many shall rejoice at his birth. (Luke 1:14)

And he shall be unto thee a restorer of [thy] life, and a nourisher of thine old age: for thy daughter in law, which loveth thee, which is better to thee than seven sons, hath born him. (Ruth 4:15)

And God blessed Noah and his sons, and said unto them, Be fruitful, and multiply, and replenish the earth. (Genesis 9:1)

PRIDE

[When] pride cometh, then cometh shame: but with the lowly [is] wisdom. (Proverbs 11:2)

Every one [that is] proud in heart [is] an abomination to the LORD: [though] hand [join] in hand, he shall not be unpunished. (Proverbs 16:5)

A man's pride shall bring him low: but honour shall uphold the humble in spirit. (Proverbs 29:23)

Pride [goeth] before destruction, and an haughty spirit before a fall. (Proverbs 16:18)

For if a man think himself to be something, when he is nothing, he deceiveth himself. (Galatians 6:3)

But he giveth more grace. Wherefore he saith, God resisteth the proud, but giveth grace unto the humble. (James 4:6)

Let another man praise thee, and not thine own mouth; a stranger, and not thine own lips. (Proverbs 27:2)

Seest thou a man wise in his own conceit? [there is] more hope of a fool than of him. (Proverbs 26:12)

[Let] nothing [be done] through strife or vainglory; but in lowliness of mind let each esteem other better than themselves. (Philippians 2:3)

The fear of the LORD [is] to hate evil: pride, and arrogancy, and the evil way, and the froward mouth, do I hate. (Proverbs 8:13)

Thus saith the LORD, Let not the wise [man] glory in his wisdom, neither let the mighty [man] glory in his might, let not the rich [man] glory in his riches. (Jeremiah 9:23)

For all that [is] in the world, the lust of the flesh, and the lust of the eyes, and the pride of life, is not of the Father, but is of the world. (1 John 2:16)

[Be] of the same mind one toward another. Mind not high things, but condescend to men of low estate. Be not wise in your own conceits. (Romans 12:16)

PROCRASTINATION

The soul of the sluggard desireth, and [hath] nothing: but the soul of the diligent shall be made fat. (Proverbs 13:4)

The hand of the diligent shall bear rule: but the slothful shall be under tribute. (Proverbs 12:24)

The sluggard will not plow by reason of the cold; [therefore] shall he beg in harvest, and [have] nothing. (Proverbs 20:4)

Boast not thyself of to morrow; for thou knowest not what a day may bring forth. (Proverbs 27:1)

Therefore to him that knoweth to do good, and doeth [it] not, to him it is sin. (James 4:17)

I can do all things through Christ which strengtheneth me. (Philippians 4:13)

Heaviness in the heart of man maketh it stoop: but a good word maketh it glad. (Proverbs 12:25)

I must work the works of him that sent me, while it is day: the night cometh, when no man can work. (John 9:4)

Let your loins be girded about, and [your] lights burning. (Luke 12:35)

But seek ye first the kingdom of God, and his righteousness; and all these things shall be added unto you. (Matthew 6:33)

Be ye therefore ready also: for the Son of man cometh at an hour when ye think not. (Luke 12:40)

He that observeth the wind shall not sow; and he that regardeth the clouds shall not reap. (Ecclesiastes 11:4)

Now no chastening for the present seemeth to be joyous, but grievous: nevertheless afterward it yieldeth the peaceable fruit of righteousness unto them which are exercised thereby. (Hebrews 12:11)

Whatsoever thy hand findeth to do, do [it] with thy might; for [there is] no work, nor device, nor knowledge, nor wisdom, in the grave, whither thou goest. (Ecclesiastes 9:10)

PROSTITUTION

Meats for the belly, and the belly for meats: but God shall destroy both it and them. Now the body [is] not for fornication, but for the Lord; and the Lord for the body. (1 Corinthians 6:13)

For whoremongers, for them that defile themselves with mankind, for menstealers, for liars, for perjured persons, and if there be any other thing that is contrary to sound doctrine. (1 Timothy 1:10)

But I say unto you, That whosoever shall put away his wife, saving for the cause of fornication, causeth her to commit adultery: and whosoever shall marry her that is divorced committeth adultery. (Matthew 5:32)

PROTECTION

No weapon that is formed against thee shall prosper; and every tongue [that] shall rise against thee in judgment thou shalt condemn. This [is] the heritage of the servants of the LORD, and their righteousness [is] of me, saith the LORD. (Isaiah 54:17)

There shall no evil befall thee, neither shall any plague come nigh thy dwelling. (Psalm 91:10)

For God so loved the world, that he gave his only begotten Son, that whosoever believeth in him should not perish, but have everlasting life. (John 3:16)

But ye [are] a chosen generation, a royal priesthood, an holy nation, a peculiar people; that ye should shew forth the praises of him who hath called you out of darkness into his marvellous light. (1 Peter 2:9)

And ye shall know the truth, and the truth shall make you free. (John 8:32)

PROVISION

And God [is] able to make all grace abound toward you; that ye, always having all sufficiency in all [things], may abound to every good work. (2 Corinthians 9:8)

But my God shall supply all your need according to his riches in glory by Christ Jesus. (Philippians 4:19)

(To the chief Musician for the sons of Korah, A Song upon Alamoth.) God [is] our refuge and strength, a very present help in trouble. (Psalm 46:1)

But seek ye first the kingdom of God, and his righteousness; and all these things shall be added unto you. (Matthew 6:33)

PURITY

Blessed [are] the pure in heart: for they shall see God. (Matthew 5:8)

BETH. Wherewithal shall a young man cleanse his way? by taking heed [thereto] according to thy word. (Psalm 119:9)

Let no man despise thy youth; but be thou an example of the believers, in word, in conversation, in charity, in spirit, in faith, in purity. (1 Timothy 4:12)

Flee fornication. Every sin that a man doeth is without the body; but he that committeth fornication sinneth against his own body. (1 Corinthians 6:18)

If we confess our sins, he is faithful and just to forgive us [our] sins, and to cleanse us from all unrighteousness. (1 John 1:9)

Marriage [is] honourable in all, and the bed undefiled: but whoremongers and adulterers God will judge. (Hebrews 13:4)

Create in me a clean heart, O God; and renew a right spirit within me. (Psalm 51:10)

For this ye know, that no whoremonger, nor unclean person, nor covetous man, who is an idolater, hath any inheritance in the kingdom of Christ and of God. (Ephesians 5:5)

But put ye on the Lord Jesus Christ, and make not provision for the flesh, to [fulfil] the lusts [thereof]. (Romans 13:14)

Mortify therefore your members which are upon the earth; fornication, uncleanness, inordinate affection, evil concupiscence, and covetousness, which is idolatry. (Colossians 3:5)

Pray for us: for we trust we have a good conscience, in all things willing to live honestly. (Hebrews 13:18)

Teaching us that, denying ungodliness and worldly lusts, we should live soberly, righteously, and godly, in this present world. (Titus 2:12)

QUITTING

I can do all things through Christ which strengtheneth me. (Philippians 4:13)

But none of these things move me, neither count I my life dear unto myself, so that I might finish my course with joy, and the ministry, which I have received of the Lord Jesus, to testify the gospel of the grace of God. (Acts 20:24)

And I will pray the Father, and he shall give you another Comforter, that he may abide with you for ever. (John 14:16)

The Lord is not slack concerning his promise, as some men count slackness; but is longsuffering to us-ward, not willing that any should perish, but that all should come to repentance. (2 Peter 3:9)

NUN. Thy word [is] a lamp unto my feet, and a light unto my path. (Psalm 119:105)

Wine [is] a mocker, strong drink [is] raging: and whosoever is deceived thereby is not wise. (Proverbs 20:1)

And let us not be weary in well doing: for in due season we shall reap, if we faint not. (Galatians 6:9)

Wherefore seeing we also are compassed about with so great a cloud of witnesses, let us lay aside every weight, and the sin which doth so easily beset [us], and let us run with patience the race that is set before us. (Hebrews 12:1)

RECONCILIATION

And be ye kind one to another, tender-hearted, forgiving one another, even as God for Christ's sake hath forgiven you. (Ephesians 4:32)

And all things [are] of God, who hath reconciled us to himself by Jesus Christ, and hath given to us the ministry of reconciliation. (2 Corinthians 5:18)

For if, when we were enemies, we were reconciled to God by the death of his Son, much more, being reconciled, we shall be saved by his life. (Romans 5:10)

And, having made peace through the blood of his cross, by him to reconcile all things unto himself; by him, [I say], whether [they be] things in earth, or things in heaven. (Colossians 1:20)

Follow peace with all [men], and holiness, without which no man shall see the Lord. (Hebrews 12:14)

Then said Jesus, Father, forgive them; for they know not what they do. And they parted his raiment, and cast lots. (Luke 23:34)

Take heed to yourselves: If thy brother trespass against thee, rebuke him; and if he repent, forgive him. (Luke 17:3)

REGRET

Brethren, I count not myself to have apprehended: but [this] one thing [I do], forgetting those things which are behind, and reaching forth unto those things which are before. (Philippians 3:13)

For godly sorrow worketh repentance to salvation not to be repented of: but the sorrow of the world worketh death. (2 Corinthians 7:10)

If we confess our sins, he is faithful and just to forgive us [our] sins, and to cleanse us from all unrighteousness. (1 John 1:9)

And we know that all things work together for good to them that love God, to them who are the called according to [his] purpose. (Romans 8:28)

And I will restore to you the years that the locust hath eaten, the cankerworm, and the caterpiller, and the palmerworm, my great army which I sent among you. (Joel 2:25)

Say not thou, What is [the cause] that the former days were better than these? for thou dost not enquire wisely concerning this. (Ecclesiastes 7:10)

Be sober, be vigilant; because your adversary the devil, as a roaring lion, walketh about, seeking whom he may devour. (1 Peter 5:8)

To every [thing there is] a season, and a time to every purpose under the heaven. (Ecclesiastes 3:1)

I have fought a good fight, I have finished [my] course, I have kept the faith. (2 Timothy 4:7)

REJECTION

If the world hate you, ye know that it hated me before [it hated] you. (John 15:18)

To whom coming, [as unto] a living stone, disallowed indeed of men, but chosen of God, [and] precious. (1 Peter 2:4)

When my father and my mother forsake me, then the LORD will take me up. (Psalm 27:10)

And he said unto me, My grace is sufficient for thee: for my strength is made perfect in weakness. Most gladly therefore will I rather glory in my infirmities, that the power of Christ may rest upon me. (2 Corinthians 12:9)

For the LORD will not cast off his people, neither will he forsake his inheritance. (Psalm 94:14)

He is despised and rejected of men; a man of sorrows, and acquainted with grief: and we hid as it were [our] faces from him; he was despised, and we esteemed him not. (Isaiah 53:3)

He that heareth you heareth me; and he that despiseth you despiseth me; and he that despiseth me despiseth him that sent me. (Luke 10:16)

Casting all your care upon him; for he careth for you. (1 Peter 5:7)

He came unto his own, and his own received him not. (John 1:11)

The stone [which] the builders refused is become the head [stone] of the corner. (Psalm 118:22)

What shall we then say to these things? If God [be] for us, who [can be] against us? (Romans 8:31)

[There is] therefore now no condemnation to them which are in Christ Jesus, who walk not after the flesh, but after the Spirit. (Romans 8:1)

But my God shall supply all your need according to his riches in glory by Christ Jesus. (Philippians 4:19)

Be sober, be vigilant; because your adversary the devil, as a roaring lion, walketh about, seeking whom he may devour. (1 Peter 5:8)

Can a woman forget her sucking child, that she should not have compassion on the son of her womb? yea, they may forget, yet will I not forget thee. (Isaiah 49:15)

RELATIONSHIPS

And the LORD God said, [It is] not good that the man should be alone; I will make him an help meet for him. (Genesis 2:18)

Be ye not unequally yoked together with unbelievers: for what fellowship hath righteousness with unrighteousness? and what communion hath light with darkness? (2 Corinthians 6:14)

Wherefore comfort yourselves together, and edify one another, even as also ye do. (1 Thessalonians 5:11)

But if they cannot contain, let them marry: for it is better to marry than to burn. (1 Corinthians 7:9)

Keep thy heart with all diligence; for out of it [are] the issues of life. (Proverbs 4:23)

[As for] God, his way [is] perfect; the word of the LORD [is] tried: he [is] a buckler to all them that trust in him. (2 Samuel 22:31)

Thou shalt not lie with mankind, as with womankind: it [is] abomination. (Leviticus 18:22)

REPENTANCE

Repent ye therefore, and be converted, that your sins may be blotted out, when the times of refreshing shall come from the presence of the Lord. (Acts 3:19)

If my people, which are called by my name, shall humble themselves, and pray, and seek my face, and turn from their wicked ways; then will I hear from heaven, and will forgive their sin, and will heal their land. (2 Chronicles 7:14)

If we confess our sins, he is faithful and just to forgive us [our] sins, and to cleanse us from all unrighteousness. (1 John 1:9)

The Lord is not slack concerning his promise, as some men count slackness; but is longsuffering to us-ward, not willing that any should perish, but that all should come to repentance. (2 Peter 3:9)

I tell you, Nay: but, except ye repent, ye shall all likewise perish. (Luke 13:3)

And the times of this ignorance God winked at; but now commandeth all men every where to repent. (Acts 17:30)

Then Peter said unto them, Repent, and be baptized every one of you in the name of Jesus

Christ for the remission of sins, and ye shall receive the gift of the Holy Ghost. (Acts 2:38)

He that covereth his sins shall not prosper: but whoso confesseth and forsaketh [them] shall have mercy. (Proverbs 28:13)

From that time Jesus began to preach, and to say, Repent: for the kingdom of heaven is at hand. (Matthew 4:17)

Or despisest thou the riches of his goodness and forbearance and longsuffering; not knowing that the goodness of God leadeth thee to repentance? (Romans 2:4)

RESPECT

Therefore all things whatsoever ye would that men should do to you, do ye even so to them: for this is the law and the prophets. (Matthew 7:12)

[Be] kindly affectioned one to another with brotherly love; in honour preferring one another. (Romans 12:10)

Honour thy father and thy mother: that thy days may be long upon the land which the LORD thy God giveth thee. (Exodus 20:12)

[Let] nothing [be done] through strife or vainglory; but in lowliness of mind let each esteem other better than themselves. (Philippians 2:3)

Honour all [men]. Love the brotherhood. Fear God. Honour the king. (1 Peter 2:17)

In all things shewing thyself a pattern of good works: in doctrine [shewing] uncorruptness, gravity, sincerity. (Titus 2:7)

Whosoever therefore resisteth the power, resisteth the ordinance of God: and they that resist shall receive to themselves damnation. (Romans 13:2)

Thou shalt rise up before the hoary head, and honour the face of the old man, and fear thy God: I [am] the LORD. (Leviticus 19:32)

But when thou art bidden, go and sit down in the lowest room; that when he that bade thee cometh, he may say unto thee, Friend, go up higher: then shalt thou have worship in the presence of them that sit at meat with thee. (Luke 14:10)

Remember them which have the rule over you, who have spoken unto you the word of God: whose faith follow, considering the end of [their] conversation. (Hebrews 13:7)

But he that doeth wrong shall receive for the wrong which he hath done: and there is no respect of persons. (Colossians 3:25)

RESTORATION

For I will restore health unto thee, and I will heal thee of thy wounds, saith the LORD; because they called thee an Outcast, [saying], This [is] Zion, whom no man seeketh after. (Jeremiah 30:17)

Restore unto me the joy of thy salvation; and uphold me [with thy] free spirit. (Psalm 51:12)

For your shame [ye shall have] double; and [for] confusion they shall rejoice in their portion: therefore in their land they shall possess the double: everlasting joy shall be unto them. (Isaiah 61:7)

And the LORD turned the captivity of Job, when he prayed for his friends: also the LORD gave Job twice as much as he had before. (Job 42:10)

For whatsoever is born of God overcometh the world: and this is the victory that overcometh the world, [even] our faith. (1 John 5:4)

Therefore I say unto you, What things soever ye desire, when ye pray, believe that ye receive [them], and ye shall have [them]. (Mark 11:24)

But the God of all grace, who hath called us unto his eternal glory by Christ Jesus, after that ye have suffered a while, make you perfect, stablish, strengthen, settle [you]. (1 Peter 5:10)

Turn you to the strong hold, ye prisoners of hope: even to day do I declare [that] I will render double unto thee. (Zechariah 9:12)

For I know the thoughts that I think toward you, saith the LORD, thoughts of peace, and not of evil, to give you an expected end. (Jeremiah 29:11)

Let not your heart be troubled: ye believe in God, believe also in me. (John 14:1)

Brethren, if a man be overtaken in a fault, ye which are spiritual, restore such an one in the spirit of meekness; considering thyself, lest thou also be tempted. (Galatians 6:1)

But seek ye first the kingdom of God, and his righteousness; and all these things shall be added unto you. (Matthew 6:33)

REVENGE

Dearly beloved, avenge not yourselves, but [rather] give place unto wrath: for it is written, Vengeance [is] mine; I will repay, saith the Lord. (Romans 12:19)

Not rendering evil for evil, or railing for railing: but contrariwise blessing; knowing that ye are thereunto called, that ye should inherit a blessing. (1 Peter 3:9)

Say not, I will do so to him as he hath done to me: I will render to the man according to his work. (Proverbs 24:29)

Thou shalt not avenge, nor bear any grudge against the children of thy people, but thou shalt love thy neighbour as thyself: I [am] the LORD. (Leviticus 19:18)

See that none render evil for evil unto any [man]; but ever follow that which is good, both among yourselves, and to all [men]. (1 Thessalonians 5:15)

Recompense to no man evil for evil. Provide things honest in the sight of all men. (Romans 12:17)

And when ye stand praying, forgive, if ye have ought against any: that your Father also which is in heaven may forgive you your trespasses. (Mark 11:25)

For he is the minister of God to thee for good. But if thou do that which is evil, be afraid; for he beareth not the sword in vain: for he is the minister of God, a revenger to [execute] wrath upon him that doeth evil. (Romans 13:4)

Who, when he was reviled, reviled not again; when he suffered, he threatened not; but committed [himself] to him that judgeth righteously. (1 Peter 2:23)

If it be possible, as much as lieth in you, live peaceably with all men. (Romans 12:18)

SALVATION

Not by works of righteousness which we have done, but according to his mercy he saved us, by the washing of regeneration, and renewing of the Holy Ghost. (Titus 3:5)

That if thou shalt confess with thy mouth the Lord Jesus, and shalt believe in thine heart that God hath raised him from the dead, thou shalt be saved. (Romans 10:9)

For by grace are ye saved through faith; and that not of yourselves: [it is] the gift of God. (Ephesians 2:8)

Not every one that saith unto me, Lord, Lord, shall enter into the kingdom of heaven; but he that doeth the will of my Father which is in heaven. (Matthew 7:21)

Jesus saith unto him, I am the way, the truth, and the life: no man cometh unto the Father, but by me. (John 14:6)

Neither is there salvation in any other: for there is none other name under heaven given among men, whereby we must be saved. (Acts 4:12)

No man can come to me, except the Father which hath sent me draw him: and I will raise him up at the last day. (John 6:44)

But the salvation of the righteous [is] of the LORD: [he is] their strength in the time of trouble. (Psalm 37:39)

(To the chief Musician, to Jeduthun, A Psalm of David.) Truly my soul waiteth upon God: from him [cometh] my salvation. (Psalm 62:1)

Be it known therefore unto you, that the salvation of God is sent unto the Gentiles, and [that] they will hear it. (Acts 28:28)

For sin shall not have dominion over you: for ye are not under the law, but under grace. (Romans 6:14)

SANCTIFICATION

If a man therefore purge himself from these, he shall be a vessel unto honour, sanctified, and meet for the master's use, [and] prepared unto every good work. (2 Timothy 2:21)

And the very God of peace sanctify you wholly; and [I pray God] your whole spirit and soul and body be preserved blameless unto the coming of our Lord Jesus Christ. (1 Thessalonians 5:23)

Sanctify them through thy truth: thy word is truth. (John 17:17)

Therefore if any man [be] in Christ, [he is] a new creature: old things are passed away; behold, all things are become new. (2 Corinthians 5:17)

I am crucified with Christ: nevertheless I live; yet not I, but Christ liveth in me: and the life which I now live in the flesh I live by the faith of the Son of God, who loved me, and gave himself for me. (Galatians 2:20)

But we are bound to give thanks alway to God for you, brethren beloved of the Lord, because God hath from the beginning chosen you to salvation through sanctification of the Spirit and belief of the truth. (2 Thessalonians 2:13)

For this is the will of God, [even] your sanctification, that ye should abstain from fornication. (1 Thessalonians 4:3)

Knowing this, that our old man is crucified with [him], that the body of sin might be destroyed, that henceforth we should not serve sin. (Romans 6:6)

Wherefore Jesus also, that he might sanctify the people with his own blood, suffered without the gate. (Hebrews 13:12)

And such were some of you: but ye are washed, but ye are sanctified, but ye are justified in the name of the Lord Jesus, and by the Spirit of our God. (1 Corinthians 6:11)

Unto the church of God which is at Corinth, to them that are sanctified in Christ Jesus, called [to be] saints, with all that in every place call upon the name of Jesus Christ our Lord, both theirs and ours. (1 Corinthians 1:2)

For by one offering he hath perfected for ever them that are sanctified. (Hebrews 10:14)

Speak thou also unto the children of Israel, saying, Verily my sabbaths ye shall keep: for it [is] a sign between me and you throughout your generations; that [ye] may know that I [am] the LORD that doth sanctify you. (Exodus 31:13)

SELF-CONTROL

He that [hath] no rule over his own spirit [is like] a city [that is] broken down, [and] without walls. (Proverbs 25:28)

He that is slow to anger is better than the mighty; and he that ruleth his spirit than he that taketh a city. (Proverbs 16:32)

Death and life are in the power of the tongue: and they that love it shall eat the fruit thereof. (Proverbs 18:21)

But a lover of hospitality, a lover of good men, sober, just, holy, temperate. (Titus 1:8)

Wherefore, my beloved brethren, let every man be swift to hear, slow to speak, slow to wrath: For the wrath of man worketh not the righteousness of God. Wherefore lay apart all filthiness and superfluity of naughtiness, and receive with meekness the engrafted word, which is able to save your souls. (James 1:19–21)

SELFISHNESS

Look not every man on his own things, but every man also on the things of others. (Philippians 2:4)

But whoso hath this world's good, and seeth his brother have need, and shutteth up his bowels [of compassion] from him, how dwelleth the love of God in him? (1 John 3:17)

Let no man seek his own, but every man another's [wealth]. (1 Corinthians 10:24)

For all seek their own, not the things which are Jesus Christ's. (Philippians 2:21)

Bear ye one another's burdens, and so fulfil the law of Christ. (Galatians 6:2)

Ye looked for much, and, lo, [it came] to little; and when ye brought [it] home, I did blow upon it. Why? saith the LORD of hosts. Because of mine house that [is] waste, and ye run every man unto his own house. (Haggai 1:9)

But to do good and to communicate forget not: for with such sacrifices God is well pleased. (Hebrews 13:16)

Let us not be desirous of vain glory, provoking one another, envying one another. (Galatians 5:26)

No man that warreth entangleth himself with the affairs of [this] life; that he may please him who hath chosen him to be a soldier. (2 Timothy 2:4)

For where envying and strife [is], there [is] confusion and every evil work. (James 3:16)

SELFLESSNESS

Look not every man on his own things, but every man also on the things of others. (Philippians 2:4)

But love ye your enemies, and do good, and lend, hoping for nothing again; and your reward shall be great, and ye shall be the children of the Highest: for he is kind unto the unthankful and [to] the evil. (Luke 6:35)

Finally, [be ye] all of one mind, having compassion one of another, love as brethren, [be] pitiful, [be] courteous. (1 Peter 3:8)

[Let] nothing [be done] through strife or vainglory; but in lowliness of mind let each esteem other better than themselves. (Philippians 2:3)

See that none render evil for evil unto any [man]; but ever follow that which is good, both among yourselves, and to all [men]. (1 Thessalonians 5:15)

He that hath pity upon the poor lendeth unto the LORD; and that which he hath given will he pay him again. (Proverbs 19:17)

For all the law is fulfilled in one word, [even] in this; Thou shalt love thy neighbour as thyself. (Galatians 5:14)

SEX

Marriage [is] honourable in all, and the bed undefiled: but whoremongers and adulterers God will judge. (Hebrews 13:4)

Flee fornication. Every sin that a man doeth is without the body; but he that committeth fornication sinneth against his own body. (1 Corinthians 6:18)

Therefore shall a man leave his father and his mother, and shall cleave unto his wife: and they shall be one flesh. (Genesis 2:24)

But I say unto you, That whosoever looketh on a woman to lust after her hath committed adultery with her already in his heart. (Matthew 5:28)

Defraud ye not one the other, except [it be] with consent for a time, that ye may give yourselves to fasting and prayer; and come together again, that Satan tempt you not for your incontinency. (1 Corinthians 7:5)

Mortify therefore your members which are upon the earth; fornication, uncleanness, inordinate affection, evil concupiscence, and covetousness, which is idolatry. (Colossians 3:5)

Meats for the belly, and the belly for meats: but God shall destroy both it and them. Now the body [is] not for fornication, but for the Lord; and the Lord for the body. (1 Corinthians 6:13)

[But] whoso committeth adultery with a woman lacketh understanding: he [that] doeth it destroyeth his own soul. (Proverbs 6:32)

Thou shalt not commit adultery. (Exodus 20:14)

SHYNESS

For God hath not given us the spirit of fear; but of power, and of love, and of a sound mind. (2 Timothy 1:7)

Be not forgetful to entertain strangers: for thereby some have entertained angels unawares. (Hebrews 13:2)

But be ye doers of the word, and not hearers only, deceiving your own selves. (James 1:22)

But sanctify the Lord God in your hearts: and [be] ready always to [give] an answer to every man that asketh you a reason of the hope that is in you with meekness and fear. (1 Peter 3:15)

SIN

Therefore to him that knoweth to do good, and doeth [it] not, to him it is sin. (James 4:17)

For the wages of sin [is] death; but the gift of God [is] eternal life through Jesus Christ our Lord. (Romans 6:23)

For all have sinned, and come short of the glory of God. (Romans 3:23)

Behold, I was shapen in iniquity; and in sin did my mother conceive me. (Psalm 51:5)

There hath no temptation taken you but such as is common to man: but God [is] faithful, who will not suffer you to be tempted above that ye are able; but will with the temptation also make a way to escape, that ye may be able to bear [it]. (1 Corinthians 10:13)

Submit yourselves therefore to God. Resist the devil, and he will flee from you. (James 4:7)

[This] I say then, Walk in the Spirit, and ye shall not fulfil the lust of the flesh. (Galatians 5:16)

Whosoever committeth sin transgresseth also the law: for sin is the transgression of the law. (1 John 3:4)

All unrighteousness is sin: and there is a sin not unto death. (1 John 5:17)

Be ye therefore perfect, even as your Father which is in heaven is perfect. (Matthew 5:48)

If thou doest well, shalt thou not be accepted? and if thou doest not well, sin lieth at the door. And unto thee [shall be] his desire, and thou shalt rule over him. (Genesis 4:7)

Then when lust hath conceived, it bringeth forth sin: and sin, when it is finished, bringeth forth death. (James 1:15)

But I say unto you, That whosoever looketh on a woman to lust after her hath committed adultery with her already in his heart. (Matthew 5:28)

SLAVERY

Stand fast therefore in the liberty wherewith Christ hath made us free, and be not entangled again with the yoke of bondage. (Galatians 5:1)

And he that stealeth a man, and selleth him, or if he be found in his hand, he shall surely be put to death. (Exodus 21:16)

Masters, give unto [your] servants that which is just and equal; knowing that ye also have a Master in heaven. (Colossians 4:1)

Servants, be obedient to them that are [your] masters according to the flesh, with fear and trembling, in singleness of your heart, as unto Christ. (Ephesians 6:5)

There is neither Jew nor Greek, there is neither bond nor free, there is neither male nor female: for ye are all one in Christ Jesus. (Galatians 3:28)

Servants, [be] subject to [your] masters with all fear; not only to the good and gentle, but also to the froward. (1 Peter 2:18)

The Spirit of the Lord [is] upon me, because he hath anointed me to preach the gospel to the poor; he hath sent me to heal the brokenhearted, to preach deliverance to the captives, and recovering of sight to the blind, to set at liberty them that are bruised. (Luke 4:18)

He that oppresseth the poor to increase his [riches, and] he that giveth to the rich, [shall] surely [come] to want. (Proverbs 22:16)

Thou shalt not deliver unto his master the servant which is escaped from his master unto thee. (Deuteronomy 23:15)

Not now as a servant, but above a servant, a brother beloved, specially to me, but how much more unto thee, both in the flesh, and in the Lord? (Philemon 1:16)

SLEEP

When thou liest down, thou shalt not be afraid: yea, thou shalt lie down, and thy sleep shall be sweet. (Proverbs 3:24)

I will both lay me down in peace, and sleep: for thou, LORD, only makest me dwell in safety. (Psalm 4:8)

[It is] vain for you to rise up early, to sit up late, to eat the bread of sorrows: [for] so he giveth his beloved sleep. (Psalm 127:2)

Love not sleep, lest thou come to poverty; open thine eyes, [and] thou shalt be satisfied with bread. (Proverbs 20:13)

I laid me down and slept; I awaked; for the LORD sustained me. (Psalm 3:5)

[Yet] a little sleep, a little slumber, a little folding of the hands to sleep. (Proverbs 6:10)

How long wilt thou sleep, O sluggard? when wilt thou arise out of thy sleep? (Proverbs 6:9)

And, behold, there arose a great tempest in the sea, insomuch that the ship was covered with the waves: but he was asleep. (Matthew 8:24)

SPEAKING IN TONGUES

And they were all filled with the Holy Ghost, and began to speak with other tongues, as the Spirit gave them utterance. (Acts 2:4)

If therefore the whole church be come together into one place, and all speak with tongues, and there come in [those that are] unlearned, or unbelievers, will they not say that ye are mad? (1 Corinthians 14:23)

And these signs shall follow them that believe; In my name shall they cast out devils; they shall speak with new tongues. (Mark 16:17)

For he that speaketh in an [unknown] tongue speaketh not unto men, but unto God: for no man understandeth [him]; howbeit in the spirit he speaketh mysteries. (1 Corinthians 14:2)

And when Paul had laid [his] hands upon them, the Holy Ghost came on them; and they spake with tongues, and prophesied. (Acts 19:6)

Yet in the church I had rather speak five words with my understanding, that [by my voice] I might teach others also, than ten thousand words in an [unknown] tongue. (1 Corinthians 14:19)

Charity never faileth: but whether [there be] prophecies, they shall fail; whether [there be] tongues, they shall cease; whether [there be] knowledge, it shall vanish away. (1 Corinthians 13:8)

Wherefore let him that speaketh in an [unknown] tongue pray that he may interpret. (1 Corinthians 14:13)

Now when this was noised abroad, the multitude came together, and were confounded, because that every man heard them speak in his own language. (Acts 2:6)

If any man speak in an [unknown] tongue, [let it be] by two, or at the most [by] three, and [that] by course; and let one interpret. (1 Corinthians 14:27)

Wherefore tongues are for a sign, not to them that believe, but to them that believe not: but prophesying [serveth] not for them that believe not, but for them which believe. (1 Corinthians 14:22)

Wherefore, brethren, covet to prophesy, and forbid not to speak with tongues. (1 Corinthians 14:39)

For they heard them speak with tongues, and magnify God. Then answered Peter. (Acts 10:46)

STAGNATION

But let patience have [her] perfect work, that ye may be perfect and entire, wanting nothing. (James 1:4)

Not forsaking the assembling of ourselves together, as the manner of some [is]; but exhorting [one another]: and so much the more, as ye see the day approaching. (Hebrews 10:25)

Wherefore I put thee in remembrance that thou stir up the gift of God, which is in thee by the putting on of my hands. (2 Timothy 1:6)

STEALING

Let him that stole steal no more: but rather let him labour, working with [his] hands the thing which is good, that he may have to give to him that needeth. (Ephesians 4:28)

Thou shalt not steal. (Exodus 20:15)

Ye shall not steal, neither deal falsely, neither lie one to another. (Leviticus 19:11)

Treasures of wickedness profit nothing: but righteousness delivereth from death. (Proverbs 10:2)

If a man shall deliver unto his neighbour money or stuff to keep, and it be stolen out of the man's house; if the thief be found, let him pay double. (Exodus 22:7)

For this, Thou shalt not commit adultery, Thou shalt not kill, Thou shalt not steal, Thou shalt not bear false witness, Thou shalt not covet; and if [there be] any other commandment, it is briefly comprehended in this saying, namely, Thou shalt love thy neighbour as thyself. (Romans 13:9)

For the love of money is the root of all evil: which while some coveted after, they have erred from the faith, and pierced themselves through with many sorrows. (1 Timothy 6:10)

Lying lips [are] abomination to the LORD: but they that deal truly [are] his delight. (Proverbs 12:22)

Thou knowest the commandments, Do not commit adultery, Do not kill, Do not steal, Do not bear false witness, Defraud not, Honour thy father and mother. (Mark 10:19)

Trust not in oppression, and become not vain in robbery: if riches increase, set not your heart [upon them]. (Psalm 62:10)

The thief cometh not, but for to steal, and to kill, and to destroy: I am come that they might have life, and that they might have [it] more abundantly. (John 10:10)

If a soul sin, and commit a trespass against the LORD, and lie unto his neighbour in that which was delivered him to keep, or in fellowship, or in a thing taken away by violence, or hath deceived his neighbor. (Leviticus 6:2)

And Zacchaeus stood, and said unto the Lord; Behold, Lord, the half of my goods I give to the poor; and if I have taken any thing from any man by false accusation, I restore [him] fourfold. (Luke 19:8)

STEWARDSHIP

As every man hath received the gift, [even so] minister the same one to another, as good stewards of the manifold grace of God. (1 Peter 4:10)

And God blessed them, and God said unto them, Be fruitful, and multiply, and replenish the earth, and subdue it: and have dominion over the fish of the sea, and over the fowl of the air, and over every living thing that moveth upon the earth. (Genesis 1:28)

And whatsoever ye do, do [it] heartily, as to the Lord, and not unto men. (Colossians 3:23)

If therefore ye have not been faithful in the unrighteous mammon, who will commit to your trust the true [riches]? (Luke 16:11)

Commit thy works unto the LORD, and thy thoughts shall be established. (Proverbs 16:3)

John answered and said, A man can receive nothing, except it be given him from heaven. (John 3:27)

For a bishop must be blameless, as the steward of God; not selfwilled, not soon angry, not given to wine, no striker, not given to filthy lucre. (Titus 1:7)

For which of you, intending to build a tower, sitteth not down first, and counteth the cost, whether he have [sufficient] to finish [it]? (Luke 14:28)

A good [man] leaveth an inheritance to his children's children: and the wealth of the sinner [is] laid up for the just. (Proverbs 13:22)

And many of them said, He hath a devil, and is mad; why hear ye him? (John 10:20)

Bring ye all the tithes into the storehouse, that there may be meat in mine house, and prove me now herewith, saith the LORD of hosts, if I will not open you the windows of heaven, and pour you out a blessing, that [there shall] not [be room] enough [to receive it]. (Malachi 3:10)

[There is] treasure to be desired and oil in the dwelling of the wise; but a foolish man spendeth it up. (Proverbs 21:20)

STORMS

Be strong and of a good courage, fear not, nor be afraid of them: for the LORD thy God, he [it is] that doth go with thee; he will not fail thee, nor forsake thee. (Deuteronomy 31:6)

He maketh the storm a calm, so that the waves thereof are still. (Psalm 107:29)

The LORD [is] good, a strong hold in the day of trouble; and he knoweth them that trust in him. (Nahum 1:7)

And he said unto me, My grace is sufficient for thee: for my strength is made perfect in weakness. Most gladly therefore will I rather glory in my infirmities, that the power of Christ may rest upon me. (2 Corinthians 12:9)

But my God shall supply all your need according to his riches in glory by Christ Jesus. (Philippians 4:19)

And when neither sun nor stars in many days appeared, and no small tempest lay on [us], all hope that we should be saved was then taken away. (Acts 27:20)

For our light affliction, which is but for a moment, worketh for us a far more exceeding [and] eternal weight of glory. (2 Corinthians 4:17)

But rejoice, inasmuch as ye are partakers of Christ's sufferings; that, when his glory shall be revealed, ye may be glad also with exceeding joy. (1 Peter 4:13)

Be still, and know that I [am] God: I will be exalted among the heathen, I will be exalted in the earth. (Psalm 46:10)

STRESS

Be careful for nothing; but in every thing by prayer and supplication with thanksgiving let your requests be made known unto God. (Philippians 4:6)

Peace I leave with you, my peace I give unto you: not as the world giveth, give I unto you. Let not your heart be troubled, neither let it be afraid. (John 14:27)

Cast thy burden upon the LORD, and he shall sustain thee: he shall never suffer the righteous to be moved. (Psalm 55:22)

Heaviness in the heart of man maketh it stoop: but a good word maketh it glad. (Proverbs 12:25)

What shall we then say to these things? If God [be] for us, who [can be] against us? (Romans 8:31)

And we know that all things work together for good to them that love God, to them who are the called according to [his] purpose. (Romans 8:28)

Blessed [is] the man that endureth temptation: for when he is tried, he shall receive the crown of life, which the Lord hath promised to them that love him. (James 1:12)

Which of you by taking thought can add one cubit unto his stature? (Matthew 6:27)

But seek ye first the kingdom of God, and his righteousness; and all these things shall be added unto you. (Matthew 6:33)

Take therefore no thought for the morrow: for the morrow shall take thought for the things of itself. Sufficient unto the day [is] the evil thereof. (Matthew 6:34)

Wherefore seeing we also are compassed about with so great a cloud of witnesses, let us lay aside every weight, and the sin which doth so easily beset [us], and let us run with patience the race that is set before us. (Hebrews 12:1)

STUDYING

Thy word have I hid in mine heart, that I might not sin against thee. (Psalm 119:11)

NUN. Thy word [is] a lamp unto my feet, and a light unto my path. (Psalm 119:105)

Study to shew thyself approved unto God, a workman that needeth not to be ashamed, rightly dividing the word of truth. (2 Timothy 2:15)

But sanctify the Lord God in your hearts: and [be] ready always to [give] an answer to every man that asketh you a reason of the hope that is in you with meekness and fear. (1 Peter 3:15)

BETH. Wherewithal shall a young man cleanse his way? by taking heed [thereto] according to thy word. (Psalm 119:9)

And be not conformed to this world: but be ye transformed by the renewing of your mind, that ye may prove what [is] that good, and acceptable, and perfect, will of God. (Romans 12:2)

These were more noble than those in Thessalonica, in that they received the word with all readiness of mind, and searched the scriptures daily, whether those things were so. (Acts 17:11)

For the word of God [is] quick, and powerful, and sharper than any twoedged sword, piercing even to the dividing asunder of soul and spirit, and of the joints and marrow, and [is] a discerner of the thoughts and intents of the heart. (Hebrews 4:12)

And Philip ran thither to [him], and heard him read the prophet Esaias, and said, Understandest thou what thou readest? (Acts 8:30)

But be ye doers of the word, and not hearers only, deceiving your own selves. (James 1:22)

And ye shall know the truth, and the truth shall make you free. (John 8:32)

SUBMISSION

Obey them that have the rule over you, and submit yourselves: for they watch for your souls, as they that must give account, that they may do it with joy, and not with grief: for that [is] unprofitable for you. (Hebrews 13:17)

Submitting yourselves one to another in the fear of God. (Ephesians 5:21)

Submit yourselves therefore to God. Resist the devil, and he will flee from you. (James 4:7)

Saying, Father, if thou be willing, remove this cup from me: nevertheless not my will, but thine, be done. (Luke 22:42)

Therefore as the church is subject unto Christ, so [let] the wives [be] to their own husbands in every thing. (Ephesians 5:24)

Husbands, love your wives, even as Christ also loved the church, and gave himself for it. (Ephesians 5:25)

Likewise, ye younger, submit yourselves unto the elder. Yea, all [of you] be subject one to another, and be clothed with humility: for God resisteth the proud, and giveth grace to the humble. (1 Peter 5:5)

Let your women keep silence in the churches: for it is not permitted unto them to speak; but [they are commanded] to be under obedience, as also saith the law. (1 Corinthians 14:34)

Wives, submit yourselves unto your own husbands, as unto the Lord. (Ephesians 5:22)

SUFFERING

But the God of all grace, who hath called us unto his eternal glory by Christ Jesus, after that ye have suffered a while, make you perfect, stablish, strengthen, settle [you]. (1 Peter 5:10)

For I reckon that the sufferings of this present time [are] not worthy [to be compared] with the glory which shall be revealed in us. (Romans 8:18)

These things I have spoken unto you, that in me ye might have peace. In the world ye shall have tribulation: but be of good cheer; I have overcome the world. (John 16:33)

And God shall wipe away all tears from their eyes; and there shall be no more death, neither sorrow, nor crying, neither shall there be any more pain: for the former things are passed away. (Revelation 21:4)

When thou passest through the waters, I [will be] with thee; and through the rivers, they shall not overflow thee: when thou walkest through the fire, thou shalt not be burned; neither shall the flame kindle upon thee. (Isaiah 43:2)

Yea, and all that will live godly in Christ Jesus shall suffer persecution. (2 Timothy 3:12)

Many [are] the afflictions of the righteous: but the LORD delivereth him out of them all. (Psalm 34:19)

SUICIDE

Be not over much wicked, neither be thou foolish: why shouldest thou die before thy time? (Ecclesiastes 7:17)

For I know the thoughts that I think toward you, saith the LORD, thoughts of peace, and not of evil, to give you an expected end. (Jeremiah 29:11)

For ye are bought with a price: therefore glorify God in your body, and in your spirit, which are God's. (1 Corinthians 6:20)

If any man defile the temple of God, him shall God destroy; for the temple of God is holy, which [temple] ye are. (1 Corinthians 3:17)

He healeth the broken in heart, and bindeth up their wounds. (Psalm 147:3)

He that loveth his life shall lose it; and he that hateth his life in this world shall keep it unto life eternal. (John 12:25)

I call heaven and earth to record this day against you, [that] I have set before you life and death, blessing and cursing: therefore choose life, that both thou and thy seed may live. (Deuteronomy 30:19)

And he said unto me, My grace is sufficient for thee: for my strength is made perfect in weakness. Most gladly therefore will I rather glory in my infirmities, that the power of Christ may rest upon me. (2 Corinthians 12:9)

For whosoever shall call upon the name of the Lord shall be saved. (Romans 10:13)

And I give unto them eternal life; and they shall never perish, neither shall any [man] pluck them out of my hand. (John 10:28)

TALENT

For we are his workmanship, created in Christ Jesus unto good works, which God hath before ordained that we should walk in them. (Ephesians 2:10)

And unto one he gave five talents, to another two, and to another one; to every man according to his several ability; and straightway took his journey. (Matthew 25:15)

For as we have many members in one body, and all members have not the same office. (Romans 12:4)

TAXES

Let every soul be subject unto the higher powers. For there is no power but of God: the powers that be are ordained of God. (Romans 13:1)

Notwithstanding, lest we should offend them, go thou to the sea, and cast an hook, and take up the fish that first cometh up; and when thou hast opened his mouth, thou shalt find a piece of money: that take, and give unto them for me and thee. (Matthew 17:27)

Tell us therefore, What thinkest thou? Is it lawful to give tribute unto Caesar, or not? But Jesus perceived their wickedness, and said, Why tempt ye me, [ye] hypocrites? Shew me the tribute money. And they brought unto him a penny. And he saith unto them, Whose [is] this image and superscription? They say unto him, Caesar's. Then saith he unto them, Render therefore unto Caesar the things which are Caesar's; and unto God the things that are God's. (Matthew 22:17–21)

TIME

But, beloved, be not ignorant of this one thing, that one day [is] with the Lord as a thousand years, and a thousand years as one day. (2 Peter 3:8)

So teach [us] to number our days, that we may apply [our] hearts unto wisdom. (Psalm 90:12)

A man's heart deviseth his way: but the LORD directeth his steps. (Proverbs 16:9)

For I know the thoughts that I think toward you, saith the LORD, thoughts of peace, and not of evil, to give you an expected end. (Jeremiah 29:11)

Whereas ye know not what [shall be] on the morrow. For what [is] your life? It is even a vapour, that appeareth for a little time, and then vanisheth away. (James 4:14)

That in the dispensation of the fulness of times he might gather together in one all things in Christ, both which are in heaven, and which are on earth; [even] in him. (Ephesians 1:10)

Commit thy works unto the LORD, and thy thoughts shall be established. (Proverbs 16:3)

My times [are] in thy hand: deliver me from the hand of mine enemies, and from them that persecute me. (Psalms 31:15)

(For he saith, I have heard thee in a time accepted, and in the day of salvation have I succoured thee: behold, now [is] the accepted time; behold, now [is] the day of salvation.) (2 Corinthians 6:2)

But of that day and [that] hour knoweth no man, no, not the angels which are in heaven, neither the Son, but the Father. (Mark 13:32)

TITHING

Bring ye all the tithes into the storehouse, that there may be meat in mine house, and prove me now herewith, saith the LORD of hosts, if I will not open you the windows of heaven, and pour you out a blessing, that [there shall] not [be room] enough [to receive it]. (Malachi 3:10)

Will a man rob God? Yet ye have robbed me. But ye say, Wherein have we robbed thee? In tithes and offerings. (Malachi 3:8)

Every man according as he purposeth in his heart, [so let him give]; not grudgingly, or of necessity: for God loveth a cheerful giver. (2 Corinthians 9:7)

But woe unto you, Pharisees! for ye tithe mint and rue and all manner of herbs, and pass over judgment and the love of God: these ought ye to have done, and not to leave the other undone. (Luke 11:42)

Honour the LORD with thy substance, and with the firstfruits of all thine increase. (Proverbs 3:9)

And blessed be the most high God, which hath delivered thine enemies into thy hand. And he gave him tithes of all. (Genesis 14:20)

Woe unto you, scribes and Pharisees, hypocrites! for ye pay tithe of mint and anise and cummin, and have omitted the weightier [matters] of the law, judgment, mercy, and faith: these ought ye to have done, and not to leave the other undone. (Matthew 23:23)

When thou hast made an end of tithing all the tithes of thine increase the third year, [which is] the year of tithing, and hast given [it] unto the Levite, the stranger, the fatherless, and the widow, that they may eat within thy gates, and be filled. (Deuteronomy 26:12)

And all the tithe of the land, [whether] of the seed of the land, [or] of the fruit of the tree, [is] the LORD'S: [it is] holy unto the LORD. (Leviticus 27:30)

TRUST

Trust in the LORD with all thine heart; and lean not unto thine own understanding. (Proverbs 3:5)

For I know the thoughts that I think toward you, saith the LORD, thoughts of peace, and not of evil, to give you an expected end. (Jeremiah 29:11)

There is no fear in love; but perfect love casteth out fear: because fear hath torment. He that feareth is not made perfect in love. (1 John 4:18)

Therefore I say unto you, What things soever ye desire, when ye pray, believe that ye receive [them], and ye shall have [them]. (Mark 11:24)

But I have trusted in thy mercy; my heart shall rejoice in thy salvation. (Psalm 13:5)

Blessed [is] that man that maketh the LORD his trust, and respecteth not the proud, nor such as turn aside to lies. (Psalm 40:4)

Commit thy way unto the LORD; trust also in him; and he shall bring [it] to pass. (Psalm 37:5)

In all thy ways acknowledge him, and he shall direct thy paths. (Proverbs 3:6)

VANITY

Favour [is] deceitful, and beauty [is] vain: [but] a woman [that] feareth the LORD, she shall be praised. (Proverbs 31:30)

Turn away mine eyes from beholding vanity; [and] quicken thou me in thy way. (Psalm 119:37)

But the LORD said unto Samuel, Look not on his countenance, or on the height of his stature; because I have refused him: for [the LORD seeth] not as man seeth; for man looketh on the outward appearance, but the LORD looketh on the heart. (1 Samuel 16:7)

He that loveth silver shall not be satisfied with silver; nor he that loveth abundance with increase: this [is] also vanity. (Ecclesiastes 5:10)

For bodily exercise profiteth little: but godliness is profitable unto all things, having promise of the life that now is, and of that which is to come. (1 Timothy 4:8)

And [when] thou [art] spoiled, what wilt thou do? Though thou clothest thyself with crimson, though thou deckest thee with ornaments of gold, though thou rentest thy face with painting, in vain shalt thou make thyself fair; [thy] lovers will despise thee, they will seek thy life. (Jeremiah 4:30)

Then I looked on all the works that my hands had wrought, and on the labour that I had laboured to do: and, behold, all [was] vanity and vexation of spirit, and [there was] no profit under the sun. (Ecclesiastes 2:11)

[Let your] conversation [be] without covetousness; [and be] content with such things as ye have: for he hath said, I will never leave thee, nor forsake thee. (Hebrews 13:5)

Vanity of vanities, saith the Preacher, vanity of vanities; all [is] vanity. (Ecclesiastes 1:2)

And be not conformed to this world: but be ye transformed by the renewing of your mind, that ye may prove what [is] that good, and acceptable, and perfect, will of God. (Romans 12:2)

VICTORY

For the LORD your God [is] he that goeth with you, to fight for you against your enemies, to save you. (Deuteronomy 20:4)

I can do all things through Christ which strengtheneth me. (Philippians 4:13)

These things I have spoken unto you, that in me ye might have peace. In the world ye shall have tribulation: but be of good cheer; I have overcome the world. (John 16:33)

Through God we shall do valiantly: for he [it is that] shall tread down our enemies. (Psalm 108:13)

There hath no temptation taken you but such as is common to man: but God [is] faithful, who will not suffer you to be tempted above that ye are able; but will with the temptation also make a way to escape, that ye may be able to bear [it]. (1 Corinthians 10:13)

But thanks [be] to God, which giveth us the victory through our Lord Jesus Christ. (1 Corinthians 15:57)

Wherefore take unto you the whole armour of God, that ye may be able to withstand in the evil day, and having done all, to stand. (Ephesians 6:13)

Finally, my brethren, be strong in the Lord, and in the power of his might. (Ephesians 6:10)

For a just [man] falleth seven times, and riseth up again: but the wicked shall fall into mischief. (Proverbs 24:16)

But the Comforter, [which is] the Holy Ghost, whom the Father will send in my name, he shall teach you all things, and bring all things to your remembrance, whatsoever I have said unto you. (John 14:26)

And I heard a loud voice saying in heaven, Now is come salvation, and strength, and the kingdom of our God, and the power of his Christ: for the accuser of our brethren is cast down, which accused them before our God day and night. (Revelation 12:10)

VIOLENCE

The LORD trieth the righteous: but the wicked and him that loveth violence his soul hateth. (Psalm 11:5)

Violence shall no more be heard in thy land, wasting nor destruction within thy borders; but thou shalt call thy walls Salvation, and thy gates Praise. (Isaiah 60:18)

Envy thou not the oppressor, and choose none of his ways. (Proverbs 3:31)

For we know him that hath said, Vengeance [belongeth] unto me, I will recompense, saith the Lord. And again, The Lord shall judge his people. (Hebrews 10:30)

For he is the minister of God to thee for good. But if thou do that which is evil, be afraid; for he beareth not the sword in vain: for he is the minister of God, a revenger to [execute] wrath upon him that doeth evil. (Romans 13:4)

Him that is weak in the faith receive ye, [but] not to doubtful disputations. (Romans 14:1)

To speak evil of no man, to be no brawlers, [but] gentle, shewing all meekness unto all men. (Titus 3:2)

Not given to wine, no striker, not greedy of filthy lucre; but patient, not a brawler, not covetous. (1 Timothy 3:3)

([A Psalm] of David.) Blessed [be] the LORD my strength, which teacheth my hands to war, [and] my fingers to fight. (Psalm 144:1)

Let death seize upon them, [and] let them go down quick into hell: for wickedness [is] in their dwellings, [and] among them. (Psalm 55:15)

VISION

And the LORD answered me, and said, Write the vision, and make [it] plain upon tables, that he may run that readeth it. (Habakkuk 2:2)

Where [there is] no vision, the people perish: but he that keepeth the law, happy [is] he. (Proverbs 29:18)

For the vision [is] yet for an appointed time, but at the end it shall speak, and not lie: though it tarry, wait for it; because it will surely come, it will not tarry. (Habakkuk 2:3)

And it shall come to pass afterward, [that] I will pour out my spirit upon all flesh; and your sons and your daughters shall prophesy, your old men shall dream dreams, your young men shall see visions (Joel 2:28)

For I know the thoughts that I think toward you, saith the LORD, thoughts of peace, and not of evil, to give you an expected end. (Jeremiah 29:11)

Surely the Lord GOD will do nothing, but he revealeth his secret unto his servants the prophets. (Amos 3:7)

Then spake the Lord to Paul in the night by a vision, Be not afraid, but speak, and hold not thy peace. (Acts 18:9)

Beloved, believe not every spirit, but try the spirits whether they are of God: because many false prophets are gone out into the world. (1 John 4:1)

Thus saith the LORD of hosts, Hearken not unto the words of the prophets that prophesy unto you: they make you vain: they speak a vision of their own heart, [and] not out of the mouth of the LORD. (Jeremiah 23:16)

And it shall come to pass in the last days, saith God, I will pour out of my Spirit upon all flesh: and your sons and your daughters shall prophesy, and your young men shall see visions, and your old men shall dream dreams. (Acts 2:17)

And he said, Hear now my words: If there be a prophet among you, [I] the LORD will make myself known unto him in a vision, [and] will speak unto him in a dream. (Numbers 12:6)

And the child Samuel ministered unto the LORD before Eli. And the word of the LORD was precious in those days; [there was] no open vision. (1 Samuel 3:1)

WISDOM

If any of you lack wisdom, let him ask of God, that giveth to all [men] liberally, and upbraideth not; and it shall be given him. (James 1:5)

But the wisdom that is from above is first pure, then peaceable, gentle, [and] easy to be intreated, full of mercy and good fruits, without partiality, and without hypocrisy. (James 3:17)

The way of a fool [is] right in his own eyes: but he that hearkeneth unto counsel [is] wise. (Proverbs 12:15)

[It is] as sport to a fool to do mischief: but a man of understanding hath wisdom. (Proverbs 10:23)

The heart of the prudent getteth knowledge; and the ear of the wise seeketh knowledge. (Proverbs 18:15)

Hear counsel, and receive instruction, that thou mayest be wise in thy latter end. (Proverbs 19:20)

Let the word of Christ dwell in you richly in all wisdom; teaching and admonishing one another in psalms and hymns and spiritual songs, singing with grace in your hearts to the Lord. (Colossians 3:16)

For I will give you a mouth and wisdom, which all your adversaries shall not be able to gainsay nor resist. (Luke 21:15)

CPSIA information can be obtained
at www.ICGtesting.com
Printed in the USA
LVHW031055130421
684340LV00008B/215